Investing Worldwide

Palm Beach, Florida
February 27 - March 1, 1990

Sponsored by the
Association for Investment
Management and Research
and the
International Society of
Financial Analysts

An *AIMR* publication

To obtain a Catalog of Publications or to order additional copies of this publication, contact:

Association for Investment Management and Research
P.O. Box 7947
Charlottesville, VA 22906
1-804-977-5724 (Phone)
1-804-977-0350 (Fax)

The Association for Investment Management and Research comprises the Institute of Chartered Financial Analysts and The Financial Analysts Federation. The International Society of Financial Analysts is a society of the Financial Analysts Federation.

This publication is designed to provide accurate and authoritative information in regard to the subject matter covered. It is sold with the understanding that the publisher is not engaged in rendering legal, accounting, or other professional service. If legal advice or other expert assistance is required, the services of a competent professional should be sought.

From a Declaration of Principles jointly adopted by a Committee of the American Bar Association and a Committee of Publishers.

Katrina F. Sherrerd, CFA, Managing Editor
Joni L. Tomal, Associate Editor
Diane B. Hamshar, Typesetting/Layout

ISBN 1-879087-03-0

Printed in the United States of America

10/30/90

Table of Contents

Foreword v

Dirty Secrets of International Investing 1
    R. Jeremy Grantham

International Investing Practices of Large
Corporate Pension Funds 9
    Robert E. Angelica, CFA

Portfolio Approaches to Global Investing 15
    Alan M. Rubenstein

Researching Non-U.S. Companies, Part I 21
    Vinod B. Bavishi, CFA

Researching Non-U.S. Companies, Part II 33
    Stephen E. Bepler, CFA

Quantitative Techniques for Portfolio
Management, Part I 43
    William E. Jacques, CFA

Quantitative Techniques for Portfolio
Management, Part II 49
    Andrew Rudd

What Went Wrong with Perestroika? 61
    Marshall Goldman

Foreword

We are pleased to publish *Investing Worldwide*, a collection of selected presentations from the conference sponsored by the Association for Investment Management and Research and the International Society of Financial Analysts.

When you put a conference together, you live in trepidation that it may bomb. We had invited many non-U.S. investors. Many of our speakers were also coming from abroad so that the program would benefit from a true international flair. The conference was to be held at a world-class resort hotel, The Breakers in Palm Beach. We even limited registrations to encourage camaraderie.

That first "Investing Worldwide" was significantly oversubscribed. Participants' evaluations after the conference, to our delight, told us that the content was fresh, practical, and well presented. The recipe worked, thank heavens!

This published collection will give you an indication of the quality of content and depth of the conference. We hope you will find this publication a valuable contribution to your knowledge of global investing.

"Investing Worldwide II" will be held on February 11-13, 1991, at the Ritz Carlton, just south of Los Angeles at Laguna Niguel. The topics and speakers will reflect changes in the global investing environment, and the format will be altered slightly to respond to last year's suggested improvements.

We hope you both enjoy and gain from reading these presentations. Let us know what you think. We hope to see you at "Investing Worldwide II."

Arnold S. Wood
President
International Society of Financial Analysts

Dirty Secrets of International Investing

R. Jeremy Grantham
Partner
Grantham, Mayo, Van Otterloo & Company

There are several unpleasant truths, what I call "dirty secrets," about global stock investing. Some of the points I have to make today are not very dirty, and some are not all that secret to international managers. They are, however, issues that managers tend to keep quiet, particularly from clients.

Diversification and Growth

The first dirty secret is that the reasons for investing internationally are not as strong as many people want us to believe. Diversification is probably the principal reason most people choose to invest internationally. I think diversification is exaggereated as a benefit of international investing. Clients think diversification will protect their assets in really terrible times. Most people agree that October 1987 or January 1990 were pretty terrible. In October 1987 the U.S. equity market collapsed, allegedly because of a specific U.S. problem—program trading. Yet, foreign markets collapsed in sympathy. Not much diversification here; in fact, a bitter disappointment on that front. More recently, the U.S. stock market got off to a terrible start this year, and thanks to Japan the year also started very badly for the EAFE (Europe, Asia, and Far East) Index.

The second reason for investing internationally is to obtain higher growth rates. Many of the assumptions underlying the view that foreign growth is higher than domestic growth are not reasonable. Growth estimates ignore heavy dilution from share issues, rights, and so forth. The remarkable recent gains relative to the United States have been largely a price/earnings (P/E) play—foreign markets are moving from a lower relative P/E (traditional relation) to a higher relative P/E (current relation).

Over the past 20 years, non-U.S., non-Japanese markets—that is, the capitalization-weighted EAFE Index without Japan—have performed exactly the same as the U.S. market. The dramatic increase in the EAFE Index has come entirely from increases in Japan. Sixteen countries have been about the same as the United States, and one has had a huge multiple play. If you can find a major equity market that will appreciate from 20 times earnings to 70 times earnings in a 20-year period, you will always make money.

There is slightly more earnings growth in the Pacific basin, including Japan, than there is in other regions of the world, but there is also more dilution, so the growth rate at the earnings-per-share level is no higher. There is also higher risk, which comes mainly from the fact that Japan and Taiwan are overpriced. In total this state of affairs does not support the assertion of greater growth in non-U.S. markets.

An analysis of market returns for four major markets—the United States, Japan, the United Kingdom, and West Germany—will illustrate my points about growth. The top half of **Table 1** shows the components of total return for these four countries for the 20-year period 1969-88. Looking at income plus real earnings, the United States returned 4.9 percent and Japan returned 4.6 percent. In terms of real earnings and income over 20 years, Japan has not delivered much. The United Kingdom is the unexpected hero.

The relative performance changes when currency and market adjustments are considered. The market revaluation (the P/E effect) is the largest effect: 8.6 percent for Japan, −2.3 percent for the United Kingdom, −1.4 percent for the United States, and 0.2 percent for West Germany. Returns arising from currency revaluations are not earnings driven. The botton half of Table 1 shows the same analysis for the five-year period 1984-88.

Table 1.   Analysis of Market Returns

1969-1988	United States	Japan	United Kingdom	West Germany
Real earnings growth	0.6	2.5	1.9	− 0.1
Income	4.3	2.0	5.3	4.3
Value-based return	4.9	4.6	7.3	4.2
Currency revaluation	0.0	3.0	2.2	1.8
Market revaluation	−1.4	8.6	−2.3	0.2
Total revaluation	−1.4	11.8	–0.2	2.0
Total returns $	3.4	17.0	7.1	6.3
1984-1988				
Real earnings growth	10.3	13.0	8.8	9.0
Income	3.9	0.8	4.5	3.5
Value-based return	14.6	13.9	13.8	12.9
Currency revaluation	0.0	8.3	8.4	8.0
Market revaluation	−1.0	16.5	0.0	0.8
Total revaluation	−1.0	26.2	8.4	8.9
Total return $	13.4	43.7	23.4	22.9

Source: Morgan Stanley Capital International (earnings and dividends): International Financial Statistics (inflation indexes).

Openness Matching

There are several arguments against investing internationally. One reason why many pension funds do not invest in foreign stocks is that doing so creates a mismatch between pension fund assets and liabilities.

This may be a short-sighted perspective, however. The concept of "openness matching" suggests that a pension fund should hedge its cost of living.

Because pensioners buy foreign goods, their cost of living includes the cost of importing a certain amount of foreign goods. The percentage of foreign goods in a pensioner's market basket varies by country. For example, in the United States and Japan the percentage is 10 percent, whereas in Holland it may be as high as 60 percent. The argument is that if a country imports goods to fill its market basket, it should buy foreign stocks to hedge the foreign component. This implies that the Dutch should invest as much as 60 percent of their pension assets in foreign assets and that the Japanese and the Americans should invest only 10 percent. Pension fund officers, however, often feel that their liabilities are purely dollar denominated and every foreign investment is an unnecessary risk. Of course, most foreign pension fund officers feel the same way, so that institutional investors believe that the lowest-risk investment is in their own country; therefore, local markets are worth a little more to locals than they are to foreigners. Theoretically, this should mean that all foreign markets are a little overpriced to outside investors!

Market Efficiency

Offsetting these substantial "dirty" negatives is one important positive: foreign markets are less efficient than the U.S. market, which is increasingly—in fact, depressingly—efficient. The best proof of this that I know is that our foreign equity division, manned by good professionals, not geniuses, has beaten the EAFE ex-Japan market with its EAFE ex-Japan money in each of nine years. In the United States—in any efficient market—you simply do not win nine out of nine. Simple disciplines when reasonably applied have worked in foreign markets, whereas domestically these disciplines have increasingly resembled getting blood out of a stone. Furthermore, having the flexibility of 16 countries, an investor can emphasize the least efficient and the cheapest countries in a way simply not available to a U.S. investor. In total, this creates a good opportunity for competent investors to justify the otherwise strangling costs and irritating hassles of foreign investing.

The Pros and Cons of Indexing

We are now all aware that investing is a zero-sum game—a poker game in which we struggle to inflict losses on others. In the United States, investors must pay 1 percent for the privilege of active trading. Everyone antes up, but in the long run only the very best people are going to win enough to cover the cost of playing the game. The bad players drop out of the poker game, and the unsuccessful investors drop out of the active management game—in other words, they index. Many hopeful investors are heard to say that, as indexing becomes popular, opportunities to beat it will return. Nothing could be further from the truth, for it is the suckers who drop out. The average quality of the players rises until, as I like to say, only Buffett, Soros, and you are left. Happy hunting!

I have watched with amazement how slowly indexing has grown. Other people believe it has grown quickly. I cannot explain why it is not at least 50 percent of the business now. Indexing piggy-backs off the efficiency of the U.S. market. The cost of indexing relative to active management is so low that indexers can gradually nickel-and-dime the active investors to death.

Foreign indexing is a completely different proposition. In the United States, indexing locks in a draw against a zero-sum game and it locks into an efficient, sensible market. Foreign indexing does not lock in the efficiency—it locks in the inefficiency, even the silliness, of the foreign markets, and it does so at a very high cost: it costs 77 basis points, as best we can ascertain, to run a $25 million index. Most of that is dividend withholding and custody charges. In the United States, indexing costs, at most, 5 basis points, which means that foreign indexing has a 72-basis-point disadvantage at the beginning. (In a world where stocks appear in aggregate to yield 6 percent after inflation, this means you are giving away 12 percent of your real return!)

One of the major problems with indexing foreign stocks is that foreign indexes are badly constructed. Several years ago both Royal Dutch Petroleum and Shell Oil were in the S&P 500 Index. At the time, Royal Dutch owned 80 percent of Shell Oil, but both were 100 percent in the S&P 500, which vastly overstated Shell's market value. Consider what would happen to the Shell Oil price if indexing had been as big then as it is now. Try buying 23 percent of Shell Oil when Royal Dutch owns 80 percent! This type of problem exists in foreign countries.

The Japanese market is vastly overstated because of cross-ownership. There have been some studies of the effect of cross-ownership on market values. French and Poterba show that cross-ownership overstates the market value in countries all around the world.[1] The problem can be illustrated with the following example. Take two publicly owned companies, each with a market value equal to asset value of $100 million. Assume Company A sells $50 million of stock to the public, so that now it has a market value of $150 million. Assume Company A takes the $50 million it received from the public and uses it to buy back stock from the public half of Company B. The public now owns $50 million of Company B and $150 million of Company A, or $200 million. The working assets and profits are the same $200 million, but the total market value is now $150 million in Company A and $100 million in Company B. So the market capital has mysteriously gone from $200 million to $250 million, but nothing has changed. This is what happens with cross-ownership.

The Japanese market is vastly overstated in the EAFE Index because of cross-ownership. Japan is currently said to represent 62 percent of EAFE. Adjusted for cross-ownership, Japan's share drops to 44 percent of the total. It is further overstated because of its severe overpricing. Overpricing is sometimes claimed to be an accounting "artifact," and this does explain some of it, but far from all. Basically, nothing explains the doubling of P/E since 1986, when the Japanese market mysteriously went from 29 to 58 times earnings, in a decade when its secular real growth appeared to come down from 10 percent to 4 percent.

---

[1] French, K. and J. Poterba. "Are Japanese Stock Prices Too High?" National Bureau of Economic Research, Working Paper #3290 (March 1990).

Imagine a day when legislation has perhaps put a few labor representatives on pension fund committees and Japan's stock market has collapsed. One of the labor reps brings a case against the fund for investing in a foreign index: It heavily overweighted a badly overpriced country in inefficient markets, at great cost. I would hate to be a professional witness called for the defense!

Silly Behavior

When we talk of silly foreign market behavior, we are sometimes given a lecture that we do not understand the Eastern markets, Japan in particular. They say that Americans do not understand the manipulation, the politics, the solidarity, the discipline, the accounting—the general Zen of the whole business. How, then, do these "experts" explain Japan's investment in country funds? Recently, the West German fund increased in value to a 100 percent premium fueled by Japanese buying. It did not seem to matter to investors in the West German fund that you could buy the same companies at half price in the marketplace through direct investing. The Zen spirit is that it is a closed fund and that, because we are going to buy it and hold it forever, it is always going to be worth twice the underlying asset value. Basically the big Japanese brokers said "jump" and enough of their silly clients did.

Another example of supreme silliness is the Tokyo real estate market. Real estate in Tokyo sells at 150 times the price of real estate in Manhattan, but rents are only four times as much. The ground under the emperor's palace is said to be worth as much as California at current rates. It is all supremely absurd and should reinforce our willingness to believe our own eyes in the Japanese stock market.

The Costs of Foreign Investing

The dirtiest secret of all is how much it costs to invest in foreign markets. The cost of investing internationally is 1 percent per year higher than the cost of investing in the United States. When you are dealing with a real return of about 6 percent, the 1 percent is a fearsome burden to carry. In most cases, clients are not aware of what a large piece of the real growth is chewed up by the cost of doing business in foreign countries.

Table 2 shows the approximate costs of international trading by the major countries. The market capitalization for each country is provided to show the relative size of the markets. The costs are shown for each country, without Japan, the EAFE Index, Japan only, and the EAFE Index with one-half of Japan's share. The average commission is based on what it would cost for a round-trip $250,000 ticket. The average estimated round-trip cost on the EAFE without Japan is 206 basis points. The dividend withholding is an extra cost of doing business in foreign countries; it averages 54 basis points. The costs of trading in Japan are lower: 170 basis points for a round trip.

The costs of foreign investing versus U.S. investing are shown in **Table 3.** In this case, foreign investing is the EAFE with a half-Japan weight. We

Table 2. Approximate Costs of International Trading (Basis Points)

	12/31/89 EAFE Mkt. Cap. ($ Billions)	Round-Trip Trading Taxes	Commission Paid on Two $250,000 Tickets	Typical Bid-Offer Spread (Small to Medium Size)	Estimated Round-Trip Total Cost	Annual Penalty from Withheld Dividends Not Recoverable	Never Paid
Australia	83	60	80	80	220	75	
Austria	13	50	250	100	350	15	
Belgium	39	50	120	50	220	60	
Denmark	23	50	100	110	260	20	
Finland	12	100	100	320	520	45	
France	188	60	60	70	190	45	
West Germany	224	16	80	80	176	45	
Holland	92		100	70	170	65	
Hong Kong	41	81	100	70	251	75	
Italy	94		120	30	150	40	45
New Zealand	9	16	100	80	196	75	
Norway	14		150	300	450	20	
Singapore	37	70	200	80	350	20	
Spain	63		200	30	230	65	
Sweden	63	200	60	300	560	30	
Switzerland	103	18	90	30	138	30	
United Kingdom	495	50	40	80	170	70	
Ex-Japan	1,591	44	80	82	206	54	3
Japan	2,366	30	70	70	170	10	
EAFE	3,957						
EAFE + 1/2 Japan	2,774	38	76	77	191	35	2
[United States]	$1,846						

assume 70 percent turnover in the U.S. active management category because of the different styles; this is the institutional average.

The estimated yearly cost of foreign active management with 25 percent turnover is 175 basis points, increasing to 328 basis points with 100 percent turnover. This compares to 92 basis points for U.S. active management and 5 basis points for U.S. index funds. There is not all that much that you can do about these costs. (The bad news is that if you wanted to leave Japan out, the costs rise about 25 basis points because Japan is the bargain on dividend withholding tax—it just does not pay any dividends—and its transaction costs are a bit lower than average.)

Table 3. Foreign Investing Costs Versus U.S. Investing Costs

		Trading Costs	*Custody*	*Dividend Withholding*	*Management Fees*	*Total- Year Costs*
Foreign active management	25% Turnover	48	20	37	70	175
Foreign active management ($25 million)	50% Turnover	95	20	37	70	227
Foreign active management	100% Turnover	191	25	37	70	328
Foreign index ($25 million)		10	15	37	15	77
U.S. active ($100 million)	70% Turnover	32	10	—	50	92
U.S. index		—	—	—	—	5

* EAFE with 1/2 Japan weight.
Note: EAFE ex-Japan add 25 basis points.

Source: Grantham, Mayo, Van Otterloo & Co. estimates

Political Risk

Clients should be aware that the real risk to managers is to their careers, so the real business is "gaming" the EAFE Index, or the S&P 500 Index in the United States. There are real risks, however, which differ from the risks encountered with domestic investment. I am talking about political and military risks.

Through U.S. eyes, the risk of investing in foreign markets is downplayed. But think about what has happened in the twentieth century. Remember how many stock markets were either wiped out in the past 70 years or came perilously close to being wiped out. The only major market to survive intact—so to speak—is the U.S. market. Every other serious market was taken over, defeated, crushed, its assets gobbled up and often put on trains and taken home, which is a tough way to lose your capital. The blue chip countries of 1990, like West Germany, had their stock markets wiped out at least once; Austria, Hungary, Romania, and Poland were overrun; and Spain, the United Kingdom, France, and Italy were nearly lost. Many of these disasters—war, revolution, economic slump—erased clusters of markets at a time. With this type of history, is it logical to use only the past 20 years of data as the norm?

A lot of people act as if all of this political risk is behind us—that the world is stabilized and we know exactly what is going to happen. But think: two years ago, how many of you thought the communists in Eastern Europe were going to fold up their tents and creep away? Of course, no one did. One of the most amazing things that has ever happened has just happened, and no one predicted it. The reality is that we know nothing about political risk except that it is much more unpredictable than we think.

The United States is a special place. It has vast natural resources, plenty of space, lots of people, a stable democratic system, military power to protect itself, and it is big enough not to be threatened by its local neighbors. It is beautifully isolated—from a military standpoint, a real headache to attack. The dirty secret here is that none of the differential political risk is incorporated into prices. To almost everybody's global thinking, you will find that the Korea fund gets about the same discount rate as the United States. Individuals are usually more savvy than institutions, however, and despite inertia and parochialism, individuals tend to realize that the United States is a special place, and they tend to want to put their money here. It is the "cool cat" institutions that have the flat discount rates and are not willing to pay much of a premium for the obvious grade of security in the United States.

Conclusion

To overcome the unpleasant truths of global stock investing, investors must follow three simple rules. First, use pooling. Pooling reduces the headaches associated with custody charges, errors, and trying to keep up with withholding taxes in chasing 16 countries. Better yet, it allows one to match the comings and goings of money. Instead of paying 75 basis points to get in and out, you switch 20 million pieces for nothing. It is a beautiful way of doing business, and clearly necessary in international investing.

Second, be an active investor, not a passive investor. Indexing is a bankrupt idea internationally, just as it is an elegant idea in the United States.

Third, you must not only be active, you also must win. The costs of doing business are great, and so are the opportunities. You must be one of the better players. How many people beat the EAFE Index? How many people beat a correct EAFE Index if it is done with half-Japan weight? About 10 percent. Now, if only 10 percent beat the index, and the index isn't worth doing, being good better be better than it has been recently.

International Investing Practices of Large Corporate Pension Funds

Robert E. Angelica, CFA
Director of Pension Investments
American Telephone and Telegraph Company
Treasurer
AT&T Foundation

International investing is becoming an important consideration for U.S. pension funds. In this presentation, I will discuss how I see investment practices of large corporate pension funds evolving over the next 10 years in terms of the proportion of pension assets that will be invested overseas, the asset classes in which those funds will be invested, and the types of managers that corporate plan sponsors will be hiring to run those investments. I will also comment on the currency policies of pension funds. My comments will be limited to the activities of large corporate pension funds—specifically defined-benefit plans of $1 billion or more governed by ERISA (Employment Retirement Income Security Act of 1974).

History of International Investing

Large corporate pension funds began investing internationally in earnest about 10 years ago. Some of the people who were in the vanguard of the movement actually started in the late 1970s, but most of us began in the early 1980s. At AT&T, we were spurred on by expectations of increased diversification and enhanced return. Those expectations have certainly been met—in fact, have been exceeded, in the case of the return expectations—thanks, in part, to favorable currency adjustments over the past 10 years. In terms of diversification, international investing has worked out pretty much as we expected.

As background, I will present some statistics on how pension funds have approached international investing. My remarks are based on data presented in Greenwich Associates surveys, a Frank Russell Company report on the asset allocation practices of its large pension clients, and surveys performed by the CIEBA (Committee for Investment of Employee Benefit Assets) group of the Financial Executives Institute.[1]

The overwhelming majority of international investing by U.S. pension funds is in foreign, publicly traded equities. Large pension funds are currently investing between 7 and 8 percent of their assets in international equities. For their large corporate clients, Frank Russell Company's average

---

[1]Financial Executives Institute, *Survey of Pension Fund Investment Practices.* Committee on Investment of Employee Benefits, Washington, D.C. (1990). Frank Russell Company, *International Equity Analytics.* Third Quarter Report, Tacoma, Washington (1989). Greenwich Associates, *Stress Strategy,* Greenwich, Connecticut (1990).

policy guideline allocation to international equities (versus actual investment) is a little over 8 percent; the range is between 0 and 20 percent. Thus,
it appears that these pension funds are below their guideline, either for tactical
reasons or because they are moving gradually toward a target.

Approximately 10 to 15 percent of the large corporate pension funds do
not invest internationally at the present time. Of the funds that do invest
internationally, on average, about one-third of their assets are invested
passively and two-thirds are invested actively. The passive component is
primarily in the form of EAFE (Europe, Australia, and Far East) Index funds,
although there are some other variations on that theme. The active pieces
are primarily invested with managers who have a non-U.S. or EAFE mandate; a smaller amount is invested with managers who have a global mandate
or who are regional or country specialists.

Currency management appears to be done in an active, opportunistic way,
primarily by managers who are skilled in currency management as part of
the overall investment process. There seems to be very little systematic
currency hedging of international exposures.

The allocation to international fixed-income securities in large corporate
pension funds is very small. According to the Russell survey, international
fixed-income investment represents only 0.3 percent of the average pension
fund. That statistic is a little misleading, however, because it is based on 35
Russell clients, 33 of whom had no international fixed-income investments.
Of the two clients who reported fixed-income investing, one has a policy
guideline of 7 percent and the other a guideline of 2 percent. The actual
allocation of funds to international fixed-income is a little higher—about 1.3
percent—for those two Russell clients. Most pension sponsors who invest
in international fixed-income assets do so on a substitution basis; they hold
it opportunistically as a substitute for either international equity or domestic
fixed-income.

The Next 10 Years

I believe there will be continued steady growth in international investing by
large pension funds, both absolutely and as a proportion of the total fund.
The advantages of increased returns and diversification may not be as great
as they were in the past 10 years, but pension sponsors seem to think that
there are still opportunities in the international market.

Greenwich Associates reports on pension sponsors' expectations for
returns from their international equity investments. Sponsors are not expect-
ing a repeat of returns experienced over the past 10 years, which were assisted
by some fairly favorable currency movements. Sponsors expect international equity returns to be 11.4 percent per year, compared to 11.1 percent for
domestic equity returns.

International Equity Investing

I think the greatest growth will be in international equity investing. The
growth will be evident in increasing allocations to international assets and in

the approach to international portfolio management. I will outline some of the changes that I see in this area.

Allocation to international. It is difficult to predict how much corporate pension funds will invest internationally over the next 10 years. My guess is that pension funds will increase their allocation to international equities to about 20 percent. My estimate is based on three observations.

First, in 10 years, the average pension fund sponsor will probably be behaving like the forward-thinkers of today. Today, the sponsors who are in the vanguard of international equity investments are allocating about 20 percent to international equities.

Second, the U.S. allocation to international assets may be estimated by looking at other countries' experiences. Countries that do not have legislative or regulatory restrictions on the amount of money they may invest internationally are investing about 20 percent of their assets in foreign country equities. For example, large corporate pension funds in the United Kingdom invest an average 20 percent of their assets in non-U.K. equities.

Third, one can look at the evidence from studies of portfolio optimization and asset allocation. Once again, the data support an allocation of about 20 percent to non-U.S. equities.

Active versus passive. I think the mix between active and passive management of international equities will remain the same. Passive accounts represent about one-third of the total, which is similar to the split within the domestic market.

Investment approach. In the early 1980s, the EAFE Index seemed like a pretty easy target to beat—in fact, the average active manager was able to beat it by a fairly wide margin. Most people attributed this to inefficiencies in the international markets. But things changed quickly, and the EAFE Index, for reasons structural or otherwise, began to perform better than the average active manager. Because of the difficulty in beating the index, a number of pension funds began to index. The trend may be reversing, however. Given the state of the Japanese market right now, the active managers who have been underweighting Japan may finally be vindicated.

I see two changes in the active management of international portfolios. These changes cover the spectrum of investment approaches. At one extreme, I see more use of country or regional specialists; at the other, I see more global management. Active international investors must choose between non-U.S. managers and country specialists. I think the pension funds will continue to hire generalist non-U.S. managers, but the mix will shift more toward hiring country and regional specialists. These specialists offer in-depth knowledge of the local culture and markets, but the decision on country allocations reverts back to the pension sponsor. Early in our international investing cycle, many of us did not feel that we had the expertise to make such a decision, so most of us went with EAFE or non-U.S. managers. Now that pension sponsors are becoming more knowledgeable about international investing, they will probably hire more regional and country specialists to manage their international assets.

Although it is taking longer than most of us expected, soon virtually all stock management will be global management, and U.S. managers will be viewed as specialists the same way Japanese managers are viewed as specialists. We are already seeing indications of the trend. Increasingly, we are being approached by our international equity managers for permission to invest selectively in North America—for example, in natural resources. We are also approached by our domestic equity managers, who follow international companies as part of their research of U.S. companies, for permission to invest selectively in international companies.

Currencies. There are two approaches to managing currency risk. The passive approach is to hedge all of the international exposures in the fund, or a proportion of them. The more active approach is to manage currency exposure opportunistically. Not many pension funds are doing across-the-board systematic currency hedging at the moment. Systematic currency hedging lowers the volatility of returns, but there are some concerns. At AT&T, one reason we decided to get into international investing was to diversify our currency exposure. We do not view currency exposure as a bad thing. We view our pension liabilities as real liabilities as opposed to nominal liabilities. Our goal is to provide a real standard of living to retirees. We believe it is too risky to have all of our international pension investments in a single currency that may be depreciating faster than the others relative to the basket of goods and services that we are trying to provide for our retirees.

Although the data do not bear this out, if purchasing power parity really does determine exchange rates in the long term, there may even be a natural hedge in that if inflation were high in the United States relative to the rest of the world, you would have a currency gain at the time when you need to help fund the higher liabilities. On the other hand, if inflation subsides in the United States relative to the rest of the world, you would have a currency loss, but you would not care about it very much because your liabilities would not be increasing as quickly.

Initially, the estimates of the cost of currency hedging vary widely. I am not sure that the costs would justify the reduction in the variability of international returns that hedging provides, even just looking at the assets only and forgetting about liabilities.

International Fixed-Income Investments
I see international fixed-income investing increasing over the next 10 years, although the growth will be slower than the growth in equity investing. Most pension sponsors believe that, given the relatively low level of investment in international equities currently, the greatest "bang for the buck" in terms of the marginal dollar that we are putting into international investing would come from putting it into equities. By putting more money into international equities, you can have a more salutary effect on the expected return and the risk of the fund, when you are starting from such a low level, than you can by investing in fixed-income. When the level of equities gets higher, then you may see more money going into international fixed-income.

New Areas of Investing

Several new areas of investment merit discussion. One area of opportunity is the emerging markets area. This trend has rippled out from the more marginal markets within the EAFE Index, such as Spain, Norway, and Finland, to non-EAFE markets like Portugal; then to some very small and truly emerging markets in Central and South America—Mexico, Brazil, Argentina, and Venezuela; in Asia—India, Thailand, and Taiwan; and most recently to Eastern European nations such as Hungary.

Another area of new opportunity in the international arena is nontraditional investments, for example real estate, venture capital, and leveraged buyouts (LBOs). AT&T has made real estate and venture capital investments in the United Kingdom, Europe, and Japan, and LBO investments in the United Kingdom and Europe. I think allocations to these types of assets will expand over the next 10 years as well, although certainly not to the extent invested in publicly traded equities.

Conclusion

I think that experience with international investing has been good. The base of investments is still very small, but I think it will continue to expand over the next 10 years, first in the equity area and then later in fixed-income.

Portfolio Approaches to Global Investing

Alan M. Rubenstein

Investment Director
Scottish Widows Investment Management Limited

There are numerous approaches to global investing. I will describe the approach used at Scottish Widows as an example of overseas portfolio management, in the hope you can profit from our experience.

The percentage of assets invested overseas by U.S. investors has been growing over the past 15 to 20 years, albeit very slowly. **Figure 1** shows the percentage of U.S. and U.K. pension fund assets held overseas. Compared to the United Kingdom, the average U.S. pension fund continues to lag in its allocation to international securities. Thus far in 1990, the average U.K. fund invests 26 percent of its assets overseas, compared to only 4 percent of U.S. pension fund assets.

Of course, one cannot evaluate the allocation without determining whether overseas investment pays off. **Figure 2** shows the return on four major markets—the United States, Japan, the United Kingdom, and West Germany—during the past decade. The returns are shown in both local currency and U.S. dollar terms. The huge rise in Japan, particularly in dollar terms, telescopes comparisons on the graph. In local currency terms, the U.S. market rose 227 percent, West Germany 264 percent, the United Kingdom 424 percent, and Japan 527 percent. When converted to dollars on an individual basis, the West German market rose by around 270 percent, the U.K. market rose by 280 percent, and the Japanese market increased by almost 1,000 percent. There are two messages in these data: First, over the past 10 years it has been beneficial to be in these markets, and second, you have to get the currency right.

It is possible to hedge away all of the currency risk, but in my opinion, returns can be enhanced by taking a reasonably long-term, fundamentally based currency strategy. If you are smart, you can get it very right. **Figure 3** shows what happened to a hypothetical U.S. investor who invested in the United Kingdom in 1980 and decided each year whether to hedge the currency risk. Even if one ignores the two extreme cases—that is, the two labeled right and wrong where we assume that each year an investor made a correct or incorrect decision on whether to hedge his portfolio—there is a 150-point advantage to the hedged portfolio over the unhedged portfolio. Most of us would happily settle for picking up such major trends. Many of you may say, however, that it is easy for me never to hedge anything as a Sterling-based investor because, in the end, the British always devalue. That may be so, but other nations also devalue, as **Figure 4** illustrates. This

Figure 1. Percentage of Assets Held Overseas: United States Versus United Kingdom

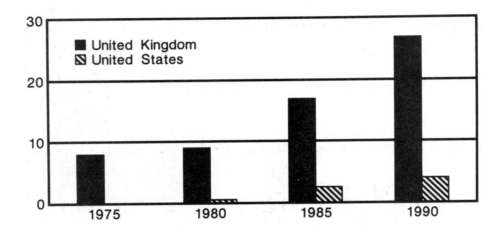

Source: The WM Company and Frank Russell Company

Figure 2.   Major Market Performance (1980-89)

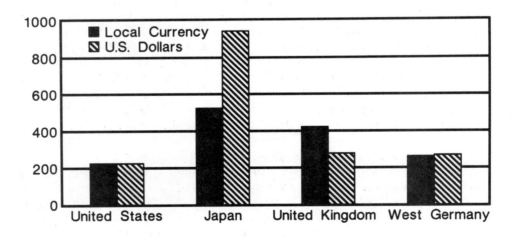

Source: Datastream International Limited

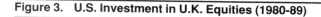

Figure 3. U.S. Investment in U.K. Equities (1980-89)

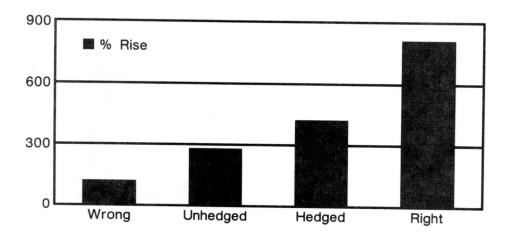

Source: Datastream International Limited

happens to be the dollar-yen exchange rate. The point is, currency should be an integral part of your investment decision.

Having decided what to do about currency, the next step is to determine the overseas asset allocation. There are a lot of sophisticated modeling techniques for asset allocation. You can base models on forecast economic growth rates, equity yields, inflation-adjusted bond yields, bond/equity yield gaps, and numerous other indicators of economic strength or market valuation levels. If you find asset allocation models too tedious or confusing, you can allocate assets between markets in proportion to the EAFE (Europe, Asia, and Far East) Index. Or, if you do not like the weighting in the EAFE Index, for example the high allocation to Japan, you can divide the assets in proportion to gross national product. The advice here is simple: Be pragmatic.

At Scottish Widows, we do not run any sophisticated asset allocation models, although we do use stock-selection models within the U.K. equity market. It is our belief that different markets are driven by different factors at different times. Models are useful tools and often help you to question your assumptions, but overdependence on a model is likely to blind you to the factors driving a market at any particular time. Scottish Widows has been successful with its strategy of over- or underweighting a region relative to an index. Clearly, the more confidence you have in your predicted outcome, the bigger the bet you are prepared to take.

Figure 4. The Dollar-Yen Exchange Rate (1980-89)

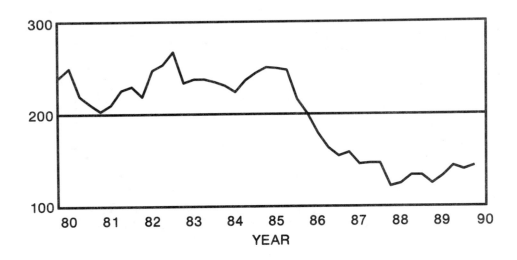

Source: Datastream International Limited

Confidence goes hand-in-hand with knowledge. I am often asked by plan sponsors or their advisors whether, for example, you need to be in Tokyo to understand how the Tokyo market works. Here I think the danger is reading "proximity" as a synonym for "knowledge." We manage a total of $20 billion worth of assets for Edinburgh, of which $5 billion are spread over 20 different countries. It is possible to manage these portfolios successfully given two things. First, we have to be prepared to visit those countries regularly, which is not as glamourous as it sounds. Second, we need to be able to speak the local language. A U.S. investor entering the U.K. market will not face too many problems. Investing in the rest of Europe or in the Far East is different. Because half of our European and Far Eastern teams are foreign nationals, we have noticed a distinct advantage in both the speed and the quality of communications.

So far, I seem to be implicitly assuming that we are talking only about equity investments. In the same way a currency decision is required and a bond/equity decision needs to be made. It is not always one sided, and there are periods—not just crisis periods such as October 1987—when bonds rather than equities offer the best returns. So in the same way that you make a bond/equity judgment in your home market, make sure you do not make a bond/equity judgment by default overseas; it has to be a conscious decision.

I have also been presupposing active rather than passive management. For those venturing into overseas markets for the first time, there must be a fairly strong attraction in concentrating on the asset allocation while using an index fund for country exposure. After all, index-tracking funds with greater or lesser degrees of tracking error exist for all the major markets and some of the smaller markets. BZW, an indexation leader in the United Kingdom, indexes the major markets and EAFE. They have been asked by clients to produce individual tracking funds for some of the larger individual European countries, such as Italy and Spain. No one has yet asked for funds for places like Malaysia or the smaller European markets, such as Switzerland. Even as a committed active manager, I might admit that in the highly rotational, highly ordered Japanese market, there is something to be said for throwing in the towel and indexing. Be warned, though: Last year, an index fund in Tokyo should have returned about 22 percent, which would have placed it in the fourth quartile of Japanese managers according to FINSTAT Statistics.

It is our belief that markets generally are not efficient. Some, particularly in Europe and the smaller Far Eastern countries, are not only immature, but demonstrably inefficient. Our approach, therefore, is one of legwork and stock picking. The approach pays off. Last year, for example, the Morgan Stanley European ex-U.K. index was up 49 percent in Sterling terms, whereas our portfolio rose by 63 percent.

Clearly, though, we did not get here overnight. Our first serious step overseas was into the United States, which was the natural starting place for us, given such factors as the size of the economy, the common language, and the time zone overlap, which are things not to be ignored. Scottish Widows first ventured into the United States in the nineteenth century, but our investments then were in bonds; equity investment did not begin until the 1940s, and it was not until around 1970 that we began to build up meaningful stakes. At that time we had to make our U.K. investments through what was called the *dollar pool*. To buy dollars to invest, you paid a 25 percent premium, and when you cashed them in, they were redeemed at par. For that reason, we used back-to-back loans to finance our investments in the United States. It also seemed natural at that time to team up with an American partner to make the stock-selection decisions for us. The removal of exchange controls in 1979 by the British government marked a turning point. We doubled our team and started running significant funds ourselves. When we were able to produce consistently better results than our partners, we knew it was time to terminate the arrangement.

Our approach to Japan was similar to our approach to the United States. Our first investments in Japan were made in the 1950s, but we sold our entire holdings in the early 1970s just before the first oil crisis. With hindsight, that was a mistake, because in 1978 when we wanted exposure to the Far Eastern markets, we had to rebuild our knowledge from scratch. Sometimes it is worth retaining some exposure, even when you have a really negative view. So our initial approach was to invest in a number of offshore funds. It quickly became clear, given the size of our intended commitment, that we would soon swamp our chosen vehicles. Therefore, to gain exposure and build our own knowledge, we decided to follow the approach we had taken in the United States and appoint two specialist managers, who would explain the reasons for every sale or purchase. Within a year we started running some funds in parallel, but as the new money came in, we invested it ourselves.

As our experience grew, the balance of power shifted, and at the end of five years we had built a sufficient track record to feel comfortable in terminating our arrangement.

Thus, the partnership approach does work. It is an ideal way to develop an operation for those who have made the decision to invest overseas but who currently lack the personnel resources or the knowledge needed for stock-selection decisions.

Interestingly, when we look back on our entry into Europe, a couple of differences stand out. We first carried out serious research into European markets in 1973, and the most active markets then were Brussels and Amsterdam. Paris represented just 1 percent of the world market, compared to 4 percent today. The liquidity of the West German and French markets has improved tremendously, and yet there are still occasions when they can be all but impossible to deal in. West Germany's one-day fall of 12 percent, and the lack of available stocks for those who actually wanted to buy in response to the 190-point fall on Wall Street last October, aptly demonstrate the problems still remaining.

Nevertheless, we felt that there was sufficient liquidity in the markets to make investment worthwhile, but we chose to invest directly. Our strategy was affected by two major factors. First, we could not find a vehicle that looked as though it would be large enough to accommodate us. Second, at that time our expertise in these markets was limited. So we invested in stocks like Deutsche Bank, Elsevier, and Heineken, where liquidity was above average. I do not believe such a strategy would work today.

We remained fairly passive investors until the early 1980s, when a number of factors came together. First, exchange controls in the United Kingdom were lifted, easing the problems of overseas investment. Second, European economies (West Germany in particular) started to recover from the recession of 1981-82. Third, governments across Europe were moving broadly to the right, encouraging share ownership. Fortunately for us, our increased activity coincided with the lift-off in European markets. It would be unwise, however, to rely on this happening again!

Overall, though, the message is simple: If you want to get overseas exposure and you want to play it safe, then index. But you can do a lot better in Europe and around the Pacific Rim by adopting an active strategy, initially in tandem with someone who knows the rules.

In summary, I offer five bits of advice based on our experience.

1. Currency does count. The difference between the hedged and unhedged returns in Figure 3 is evidence enough that it can make a lot of difference.
2. Be pragmatic. Asset allocation is not a science. Expert systems do not have the knack of telling you when they are about to break down. They will do anything you want with the numbers you give them, but make sure you give them the right numbers.
3. Knowledge and proximity are not the same thing. Make sure you buy knowledge because it is immensely more valuable.
4. Indexation does not pay (in most markets, anyway).
5. It is a jungle out there—get yourself a good jungle guide.

Researching Non-U.S. Companies, Part I

Vinod B. Bavishi, CFA
Executive Director
The Center for International Financial Analysis and Research

Researching non-U.S. companies is challenging. One of the biggest challenges is to make the financial data comparable.

The Center for International Financial Analysis and Research has been working on a research project to identify the impact of accounting differences on a country and industry level. The goal is to develop a logic of adjustments so that computerized adjustments may be made to improve the comparability of financial statements internationally.

In this presentation, I will discuss (1) why comparable financial statements should be developed, (2) the steps that are necessary to restate financial statements on a comparable basis, and (3) the limitations of restating financial statements.

Benefits of Adjusted Financial Statements

Comparable financial statements have two important benefits for portfolio managers. First, comparable financial statements help portfolio managers screen a database of potential stocks. In the old days, when portfolio managers only had to research 100 companies, it was possible to visit each company to uncover information about how the company was run and determine the specific accounting conventions followed. The world is different now. It is not uncommon for portfolio managers to select from 5,000 or more companies worldwide using quantitative measures to identify a smaller set of stocks to research. Most of the criteria are based on financial data. For example, if you are a value investor and want to look at a set of companies with low price/earnings ratios, you should make sure that the earnings figures are comparable so that the rankings make sense.

The second advantage of comparable financial statements is that they provide a global norm for comparing companies. Global portfolio managers should look at companies on a common basis; comparable financial statements are the first step. For example, if a portfolio manager wants to look at all of the pharmaceutical companies around the world, the companies must be normalized so that they are comparable. How else can one decide which companies in the same industry have the best performance?

The Restatement Process

The international accounting restatement process is a spectrum ranging from no reconciliation to a complete reconciliation (see **Figure 1**). On one end of the spectrum are numbers reported by local companies for local users under local accounting standards. On the other end are the companies that report

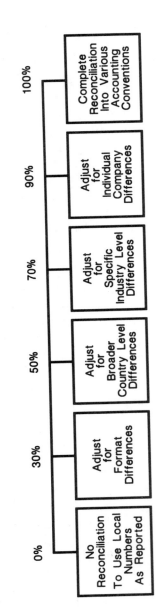

Figure 1. Spectrum of International Accounting Restatement Process: Degree of Comparability

Source: Center for International Financial Analysis and Research, Princeton, New Jersey

numbers in the standardized manner for global users. Clearly, the greater the restatement, the greater the comparability.

Restatement would not be necessary if companies followed the same accounting guidelines or were willing to restate their financial statements to conform with other countries' practices. For example, because of the large number of investors in the United States, one might think that companies would take it upon themselves to restate their financial statements to conform with U.S. Generally Accepted Accounting Principles (GAAP) to make their stock more attractive to U.S. investors. In fact, only the companies that are listed on U.S. exchanges or that issue American Depositary Receipts (ADRs) prepare reports for the U.S. audience.

There are two basic reasons why many of these companies do not have their financial statements restated: timeliness and cost. If a Japanese firm hires an accounting company to have its financial statements restated from Japanese standards to U.S. standards, there is a delay of at least one month. In addition, the restating would probably cost around $100,000. Clearly, this is not a realistic option.

If companies will not restate their financial statements, perhaps accountants and portfolio managers could agree on a uniform global accounting standard. This idea is great in theory, but improbable in practice. Picture it: The portfolio manager jumps on the idea and outlines the accounting standards, and then he goes to the beach to wait for the accountants to make a decision; unfortunately, the portfolio manager will get only a bad sunburn, because it is going to take the accountants more than 10 years to agree. There has been progress by various international accounting standard-setters to harmonize accounting standards, but harmonization has not taken place on the major issues. Thus, uniform global accounting standards do not represent a viable option in the interim.

The interim solution is to take steps toward making financial statements comparable. From our perspective, the restatement process involves the following steps: adjust for format changes, adjust for country-level differences, adjust for specific industry-level differences, and adjust for individual company differences.

Format differences. Format differences are the basic differences arising from items being recorded on the wrong side of the balance sheet (relative to the U.S. view). We have identified over 200 types of format adjustments that must be made. Some examples are given here to illustrate this point. The common practice in the United States is to use contra accounts for some offsets, such as accumulated depreciation, bad debt reserves, and Treasury stocks. In other countries, these accounts would not be contra accounts. This will lead to overstated accounts relative to the U.S. company. For example, if depreciation is not netted out against fixed assets, the fixed-asset account— and total assets—will be overstated relative to the U.S. company. In financial institutions, particularly in Europe, contingent liabilities are reported on both sides of the balance sheet, but that is not the norm in the United States or the United Kingdom. Format adjustments do not involve changing any numbers, only regrouping them to get more comparable asset, liability, and equity accounts between different companies from different countries.

Country-level adjustments. Countries differ in their accounting systems. Therefore, a number of country-specific accounting adjustments must be made. **Tables 1, 2, and 3** provide a summary of major accounting differences.

Table 1. Major Accounting Differences among Countries: Industrial Companies

Country	Revaluation Allowed	Consolidated Financial Data	Valuation of Long-Term Investments 20% - 50%	Inventory Valuation Methods
North America				
Canada	Yes	E	Equity	FIFO
Mexico	Yes	M	Equity	Rep. cost
United States	No	E	Equity	FIFO
Asia/Pacific				
Australia	Yes	E	Eq/PC	FIFO
Hong Kong	Yes	E	Cost/Eq	FIFO
Japan	No	M	Cost/Eq	Average
Korea, South	Yes	L	Cost	Average
Malaysia	Yes	E	Cost/Eq	FIFO
New Zealand	Yes	M	Equity	FIFO
Singapore	Yes	E	Equity	Average
Europe				
Austria	Yes	L	Cost	Not disc.
Belgium	Yes	L	Cost/Eq	Mixed
Denmark	Yes	M	Equity	FIFO
Finland	Yes	M	Cost	FIFO
France	Yes	M	Equity	FIFO
Germany, West	Yes	M	Cost	Average
Holland	Yes	E	Equity	FIFO
Italy	Yes	L	Cost/Eq	Mixed
Norway	Yes	M	Cost/Eq	FIFO
Spain	Yes	L	Cost/Eq	Average
Sweden	Yes	E	Cost/Eq	FIFO
Switzerland	Yes	M	Cost/Eq	Average
United Kingdom	Yes	E	Equity	FIFO
Africa/Middle East				
South Africa	No	E	Equity	FIFO

Key:

Consolidated Financial Data

E	Extensively disclosed
M	Moderately disclosed
L	Less frequently disclosed

Inventory Valuation Methods

FIFO	First in first out
Rep. cost	Replacement cost
Average	Average cost
Mixed	No majority practice, one of several methods used

Valuation of Long-Term Investments 20-50%

Eq/Pc	Equity method; partially consolidated
Cost/Eq	Cost method or equity method

(continued)

There are several types of adjustments in this category. The first type of adjustment is for differences in accounting for discretionary reserves. For example, many countries permit multinational companies to set up general-purpose reserves at management's discretion for nonspecific expenses such as "doing business abroad." For a U.S. multinational company, any risk associated with doing business abroad is considered a normal business risk;

Table 1.   Major Accounting Differences among Countries: Industrial Companies (continued)

Country	Deferred Income Taxes	Discretionary and/or Nonequity Reserves	Currency Translation Gains/Losses Taken to:	Depreciation Methods
North America				
Canada	Used	Not used	IS/Defer	SL
Mexico	Used	Not used	ND	SL
United States	Used	Not used	IS/SE	SL
Asia/Pacific				
Australia	Used	Not used*	IS/SE	SL
Hong Kong	Used	Not used*	IS/SE	SL
Japan	Not used	Not used*	IS/Defer	AM
Korea, South	Not used	Not used*	IS/Defer	AM
Malaysia	Used	Not used*	IS	SL
New Zealand	Used	Not used*	IS/SE	SL
Singapore	Used	Not used*	IS	SL
Europe				
Austria	Not used	Used	ND	SL
Belgium	Not used	Used	IS/SE	SL
Denmark	Used	Used	IS/SE	SL
Finland	Not used	Used	IS/Defer	SL
France	Used	Used	IS/SE	SL
Germany, West	Not used	Used	IS/SE	Mixed
Holland	Used	Not used	IS/SE	SL
Italy	Not used	Used	IS/Defer	SL
Norway	Used	Used	IS	SL
Spain	Not used	Used	IS/Defer	SL
Sweden	Not used	Used	IS/SE	SL
Switzerland	Not used	Used	SE	SL
United Kingdom	Used	Not used*	IS/SE	SL
Africa/Middle East				
South Africa	Used	Not used*	IS/SE	SL

Key:

Currency Translation Gains/Losses Taken to:		Depreciation Methods	
IS	Income statement	SL	Straight line method
SE	Shareholders' equity	AM	Accelerated method
IS/Defer	Income statement and/or deferred		
IS/SE	Income statement and/or shareholders' equity		
ND	Not disclosed		

* Specific items such as replacement reserves or excess depreciation used.

a general nonquantifiable reserve cannot be set up just for that purpose. Therefore, the reserves being expensed in those countries allowing such reserves should be added back so that earnings are more compatible with those in other countries.

The second type of adjustment is for differences in accounting for depreciation. In the United States, depreciation expense is relatively low because companies are allowed to use accelerated depreciation for tax purposes and straight-line depreciation for financial reporting purposes. Other countries have different rules. For example, some of the excess depreciation in countries like Japan, West Germany, and Switzerland, which have higher depreciation expenses, must be subtracted.

Effective tax rates are not comparable around the world. The biggest problem is that countries differ in their definition of tax-deductible expenses. This affects after-tax income comparisons. There are two ways of dealing

Table 2. Major Accounting Differences among Countries: Banks

Country	Valuation of Marketable Securities	Allow. Loan Losses Fixed by Law	Valuation of Long-Term Investments	Hidden or Nonequity Reserves
North America				
Canada	MV	Yes	PP	No
United States	MV	No	PP	No
Asia/Pacific				
Australia	MV	No	PP	No
Hong Kong	LCM	Yes	PP/Amort	No
Japan	LCM	Yes	PP	No
Korea, South	LCM	Yes	PP	No
Malaysia	LCM	No	PP/Amort	No
Singapore	LCM	No	PP/MV	No
Europe				
Austria	LCM	ND	PP	Sep'd
Belgium	HC	No	PP	No
Denmark	MV	No	MV	SE
Finland	LCM	Yes	PP	Sep'd
France	LCM	No	PP	Sep'd
Germany, West	LCM	Yes	PP	SE
Holland	MV	No	MV	Sep'd
Italy	LCM	Yes	PP	Sep'd
Norway	LCM	Yes	PP	Sep'd
Spain	LCM	Yes	PP/MV	Sep'd
Sweden	LCM	Yes	MV	Sep'd
Switzerland	LCM	No	LCM	Sep'd
United Kingdom	MV	No	LCM	No
Africa/Middle East				
South Africa	MV	No	MV	No

Key:

Valuation of Marketable Securities

MV	Market value
HC	Historical cost
LCM	Lower of cost or market
ND	Not determinable

Hidden or Nonequity Reserves

No	Do not exist
Sep'd	Exist and separately accounted for
SE	Exist and accounted for as a part of shareholders' equity

Valuation of Long-Term Investments

PP	Purchase price
PP/Amort	Purchase price adjusted by amortization of premiums or discounts
PP/MV	Purchase price adjusted by market value
MV	Market value
LCM	Lower of cost or market

(continued)

with this problem: Use pre-tax numbers, ignoring taxes completely, or use a marginal tax rate for each country as a substitute to avoid the idiosyncrasies that are arbitrarily decided by the company rather than based on its performance.

In some countries, intangibles are amortized over up to 40 years. In other countries they are expensed in the year in which the assets were acquired. Our suggestion would be to remove them, again trying to show the true performance.

We make adjustments for foreign currency translation gains and losses. These are the gains and losses booked at year-end because one must prepare financial statements in one set of currencies. We feel they are not economic gains and losses, and they should be transferred out so the numbers will be more comparable.

Table 2.   Major Accounting Differences among Countries: Banks (continued)

Country	Customers' Liability for Acceptances	Interest Income/Expense Disclosed	Commissions Earned/Paid Disclosed
North America			
Canada	TA	Gross	ND
United States	TA	Gross	Gross
Asia/Pacific			
Australia	TA	Gross	Net
Hong Kong	TA	ND	ND
Japan	TA	Gross	Gross
Korea, South	TA	Gross	Gross
Malaysia	TA	ND	ND
Singapore	TA	ND	ND
Europe			
Austria	TA/pt	Gross	Net
Belgium	FN	Gross	Gross
Denmark	TA/pt	Gross	Net
Finland	FN	Gross	Net
France	FN	Gross	Gross
Germany, West	TA/pt	Gross	Gross
Holland	FN	Net	Net
Italy	FN	Gross	Gross
Norway	FN	Gross	Net
Spain	FN	Gross	Net
Sweden	FN	Net/FN	Gross
Switzerland	FN	Gross	Gross
United Kingdom	FN	Net/FN	Net
Africa/Middle East			
South Africa	TA	ND	ND

Key:

Customers' Liability for Acceptances

TA	As a part of total assets
TA/pt	Partially as a part of total assets
FN	Disclosed only in a footnote

Commissions Earned/Paid Disclosed

Gross	Gross amounts on income statement
Net	Net amounts on income statement
Net/FN	Net amounts on income statement and gross amounts on a footnote
ND	Not disclosed separately

Price/earnings (P/E) ratios are often used to compare companies. Even if the earnings-per-share number is calculated consistently, however, there are still a number of different ways to calculate P/E ratios, and people naturally choose the one that presents their performance in the most favorable light. Sometimes earnings per share is not clearly defined—either for the numerator or denominator. People may use the beginning number of shares, the ending number of shares, or the average number of shares.

Results of Study

To assess the impact of accounting differences, we have studied the accounting policies of 200 companies in eight industries in eight countries. The countries are Australia, France, West Germany, Italy, Japan, Switzerland, the United Kingdom, and the United States. The eight industries are automobile, banks, chemicals, electronics, food and beverage, insurance, machinery, and industrial equipment and mining.

We did not change any numbers that contribute to the performance of the firm. We are only trying to identify arbitrary accounting choices or the tax

Table 3. Major Accounting Differences among Countries: Insurance Companies

Country	Life/Non-life by the Same Company	Fixed-Income Securities Valuation	Equity Securities Valuation	Reinsurance Business	Underwriting Expenses Disclosed	Hidden or Nonequity Reserves
North America						
Canada	No	AC	HC	ND	GAE	ND
United States	Yes	AC	MP	Net	Sep	NE
Asia/Pacific						
Australia	No	HC	MP	Gross	Sep	ND
Hong Kong	No	LCM	HC	Net	GAE	ND
Japan	No	LCM	LCM	Gross	GAE	NE
Korea, South	No	AC	LCM	Gross	GAE	NE
Malaysia	Yes	HC	MP	Net	Sep	NE
Singapore	Yes	HC	MP	ND	Sep	NE
Europe						
Austria	Yes	ND	ND	Net	Sep	Sep
Belgium	Yes	LCM	MP	Gross	Sep	Sep
Denmark	Yes	AC	MP	Net	GAE	ND
Finland	Yes	AC	MP	Gross	Sep	Sep
France	Yes	HC	HC	Net	Sep	Sep
Germany, West	Yes	AC	LCM	Net	Sep	ND
Holland	Yes	AC	MP	Gross	Sep	Sep
Italy	Yes	LCM	LCM	Net	Sep	ND
Norway	Yes	LCM	LCM	Net	GAE	Sep
Spain	Yes	HC	LACM	Net	Sep	Not Sep
Sweden	Yes	LCM	LCM	Net	GAE	Sep
Switzerland	Yes	LCM	LCM	Net	GAE	ND
United Kingdom	Yes	MP	MP	Gross	GAE	NE
Africa/Middle East						
South Africa	No	AC	MP	Net	GAE	ND

Key:

Fixed-Income and Equity Securities Valuation

AC	Amortized cost
HC	Historical cost
MP	Market price
LCM	Lower of cost or market
ND	Not disclosed
LACM	Lower cost and partial adjustment to market

Underwriting Expenses Disclosed

GAE	Part of General Administrative expenses
Sep	Separately disclosed

Reinsurance Business

ND	Not disclosed
Gross	Gross amounts on individual accounts are disclosed
Net	Only net reinsurance results are disclosed

Hidden or Nonequity Reservese

NE	Do not exist
Sep	Exist and separately accounted for
Not sep	Exist but not separately accounted for
ND	Not disclosed

Source: International Accounting and Auditing Trends. Princeton, New Jersey: Center for International Financial Analysis & Research (June 1989).

choices that companies have selected, so that in the end you can isolate true differences in performance. **Tables 4 and 5** provide the restatement logic that we utilized.

Tables 6 and 7 show what we have found so far in the major markets. The country-specific differences account for most of it, but there are some industry differences. Of the leading markets we studied, we found West Germany, Switzerland, and Japan more difficult to deal with because of the tax influence on their accounting standards. We found depreciation, discretionary reserves, and consolidation practices changing the accounting standards or numbers more than other items.

Table 4. Global Accounting Standards Used in Restatement

Current Practice and Where Used	*Method Followed by CIFAR*
Inventory Valuation	
• Lower cost or market is commonly used • Cost is by FIFO or Weighted Average Method • Sometimes a different method for a different type of inventory is used • LIFO is common in the U.S. • Current Cost is not followed in industrial countries	• Lower cost or market • Cost: FIFO (or Average Method) (Note: The difference between FIFO and Average Method is minimal if there is high turnover in inventory and low inflation) • Retail Method is accepted for retailing
Depreciation Method	
• Most of the countries use Straight Line as a standard for accounting method • In Japan it is mandatory to use a Declining Balance Method for accounting and tax purposes • West Germany uses Declining Balance at the beginning and Straight Line later	• Straight Line Method
Excess Depreciation	
• West Germany and northern European countries allow it • Usually for tax benefits	• Add them back
Consolidation of Subsidiaries	
• Not all subsidiaries are consolidated in many countries • Consolidation of financial subsidiaries with industrial operations is now required in the U.S.	• Consolidate them if information for the subsidiaries is given • Segregate them
Discretionary Reserves	
• Various types of reserves • Legal reserve in Japan, Switzerland • Excess depreciation in West Germany • Revaluation reserves in U.K., France, Italy, Holland, and Sweden	• Eliminate all reserve impacts except legal reserves in Japan, Switzerland
Deferred Taxes	
• Generally accepted except in Japan and West Germany • Partial adjustments are necessary in every country, even though their impacts are not significant	• To reflect any type of differences between tax and financial accounting
Goodwill Amortization	
• Generally capitalized and amortized • Period of amortization is very diverse • Quite a few companies take goodwill to shareholders' equity	• Eliminate goodwill and adjust shareholders' equity
Foreign Currency Translation	
• Some do not segregate between exchange gains and losses and foreign currency translation gains and losses • In Japan and West Germany, the Current Rate Method is not the same as other countries' methods	• Current Rate method • Foreign exchange gains and losses on the income statement • Foreign currency translation gains and losses to shareholders' equity

Source: Center for International Financial Analysis & Research, Inc., Princeton, New Jersey

Table 5.   Restatement Algorithm

Accounting Item	*Restatement Adjustment Needed*

A. *Discretionary Reserves*
 	
Discretionary reserves are common in West Germany, Italy, and Switzerland
	Current year:
	    DR. Income tax expense account
	    DR. Nonequity reserve account
	        CR. Reserve charges account
	        CR. Deferred tax es account
	
	Cumulative:
	    DR. Nonequity reserve account
	        CR. Deferred taxes account
	        CR. Retained earnings account

B. *Depreciation Expenses*
 	
Depreciation expenses are much higher than average in Japan, West Germany, and Switzerland
	Current year:
	    DR. Income tax expense account
	    DR. Accumulated depreciation account
	        CR. Deferred taxes account
	        CR. Depreciation exp. account
	
	Cumulative:
	    DR. Accumulated depreciation account
	        CR. Deferred taxes account
	        CR. Retained earnings account

C. *Revaluation of Fixed Assets*
 	
• Common in the United Kingdom, France, Italy, Holland, Sweden
• Varies a lot from company to company; thus, requires company-specific treatment
	Revaluation reserve is taken to nonequity reserves only if not included in shareholders' equity by the company. If nonequity reserve contains only "Rev. Reserve," it should be adjusted as follows:
	    DR. Revaluation reserve account
	        CR. Fixed assets account
	Note: Depreciation portion of revaluation is already adjusted in Item B above

D. *Effective Tax Rate* Due to variations in how taxable income and taxes payable are defined, effective tax rate is not a comparable number globally	For Global comparison purposes, two options exist: 1. To ignore tax numbers completely (to use pretax income as a numerator for all profitability ratios) 2. To use marginal corporate tax rate in each country as a fixed tax rate so that the fundamental difference in tax expense between countries has been retained but variation on a company-specific basis with the country is neutralized
E. *Intangibles* Goodwill and other intangibles are amortized differently around the world	CIFAR recommends that intangibles be removed from total assets and amortized against shareholders' equity

F. *Foreign Currency Translation Gains/Losses*
 	
• In general, taken to shareholders' equity
• If taken to income statement, it needs to be removed
	If gain:
	    DR. Foreign currency translation gain account
	        CR. Retained earnings account
	If loss:
	    DR. Retained earnings account
	        CR. Foreign currency translation loss account

G. *Consolidation of Subsidiaries* Consolidation of financial subsidiaries is common in the U.S.	To deconsolidate: debit all of the liabilities and credit all of the assets of the subsidiary except investments; vice-versa in case of consolidation

Source: Center for International Financial Analysis & Research, Inc., Princeton, New Jersey

Country	N	% Cost of Goods Sold	% Operating Income	% Net Income Taxes	% Net Income
Australia	10	NS	1	11	5
Belgium	5	1	9	NM	9
Canada	5	NS	NS	NS	NS
France	21	−1	7	9	6
West Germany	17	−2	28	40	44
Italy	5	−1	14	31	11
Japan	4	21	−5	NS	12
Sweden	5	−1	26	56	60
Switzerland	3	2	−1	4	−8
United Kingdom	8	NS	4	3	4

Table 6.   Income Statement Data Items: Changes Observed

NS = Not significant
N = Number of companies included
NM = Not meaningful

Source: Center for International Financial Analysis & Research, Inc., Princeton, New Jersey

The countries may be divided into three groups on the basis of the number of adjustments that had to be made to be consistent with a standard accounting system. The least number of changes occur with U.S. companies because U.S. accounting standards provide better numbers for interpretation purposes, having been heavily influenced by the capital markets. The next group would be the United Kingdom, Canada, Holland, and Australia, which also have very independent accounting standards and where there is input given by capital market users. The last group would be Japan, West Germany, France, Italy, and Spain, which have more difficulties because of the tax laws on accounting standards.

Limitations

The biggest limitation in efforts to restate financial statements is that there is not enough information to make the financial statements truly comparable. For example, it is difficult—if not impossible—to unravel the effects of different consolidation practices. Annual reports do not contain sufficient data. In addition, certain items are not reported in all countries around the world. For example, in some cases, depreciation expense is not listed separately.

One major limitation with the global screening approach is that the data may not be for comparable time periods. The problem is complicated by different fiscal years and the time it takes to report and restate financial statements. Each country has its own convention: Japan's fiscal year ends on March 31, and they report very fast; the year-end dates in the United Kingdom are in June or September; in countries like Italy, Spain, and Austria, reports are not prepared until six or eight months after the fiscal year-end. The result is that one could end up with 1989 data on Japan, 1988 data on some of the European countries, and 1987 data for other countries.

Finally, the usefulness of this exercise will be limited if markets are not integrated. Personally, I believe markets are still segmented—the majority

Table 7.   Balance Sheet Data Items: Changes Observed

	N	% Net Fixed Assests	% Accu. Depreci- ation	% Intan- gible Assets	%Deferred Taxes	% Non- Equity Reserves	% Share holders Equity	%Total Assets
Australia	10	−11	NS	−10	NC	NC	−11	−4
Belgium	5	−4	NS	−37	NC	NC	−14	−2
Canada	5	NS	NS	−1	NC	NC	NS	NS
France	21	−1	NS	−62	17	NC	−28	−7
West Germany	17	77	−39	−3	NM	−67	41	24
Italy	5	−25	NS	−80	45	NC	−28	−8
Japan	4	62	−31	−4	NM	NC	14	17
Sweden	5	40	−30	−16	NC	−100	44	1
Switzerland	3	−2	NS	−3	NC	NC	4	−1
United Kingdom	8	−12	1	−11	−38	NC	−14	−6

N = Number of companies included
NC = No change
NS = Not significant
NM = Not meaningful

Source: Center for International Financial Analysis & Research, Inc., Princeton, New Jersey

are going to be local users with the local data, and they have no reason to change their perspective.

Conclusion

In conclusion, I believe there will be a greater need to look at companies on a comparable basis in the next 20 years. Accounting standards will begin to harmonize. The impetus for change will come from finance directors of these multinational companies rather than from the accounting industry.

Researching Non-U.S. Companies, Part II

Stephen E. Bepler, CFA
Senior Vice President and Director
Capital Research International

U.S. investors are going international. To be successful in this endeavor, they must be able to determine where there is value in non-U.S. companies. In this presentation, I will discuss some of the critical aspects of researching non-U.S. companies.

Global Investing in the Past

I have been an analyst since 1968, and I made my first calls on international companies in 1970. The first two were Philips of Holland and Siemens of West Germany. They both sold light bulbs, but as I discovered, the similarity ended there. My experience with these two companies taught me a lesson about appearances, and more importantly, about the importance of understanding different accounting practices.

At the Philips headquarters in Eindhoven, I was cordially received in a brightly lighted room and provided with more details about the company than I could possibly remember. Philips obligingly published its reports in English and even published an addendum showing the differences between Dutch accounting standards and U.S. Generally Accepted Accounting Principles (GAAP). The atmosphere was comfortable, but just different enough to be enticing. Philips was the General Electric of Europe; at the time, its stock was selling for about 45 guilders. At the end of January this year, however—more than 20 years later—adjusting for all rights offerings, Philips was selling for only 43 guilders. So much for comfort!

My experience at Siemens, also in 1970, was totally different. In Munich, I was received in a dim room by Dr. Gunter Schone, who commented that because there was ample natural light, he hoped I did not mind if he left the lights off. (It was about 3:00 PM on a gray January afternoon.) Dr. Schone proceeded to leave me in the dark about Siemens, which he consistently did to others over the years. He was cordial to a fault, but revealed virtually nothing. Siemens was then selling for about DM 165 per share. On January 31, 1990, it was selling for DM 700, adjusting for all rights offerings.

There were obvious differences between these two companies, but I didn't correctly interpret them. Apart from the companies' very different mix of businesses, Siemens offered limited public disclosure and no guidance, and presented its results in German accounting—the analytical equivalent of Hadrian's Wall. Philips seemed to tell you what you wanted to know, but in retrospect, it was not very helpful. Siemens told you only what they wanted you to know, which was nothing, and were sparing even at that. Beyond this miserly level of disclosure, however, lay a dramatically undervalued equity.

I was too inexperienced to recognize this at the time: I recommended Philips as a buy and deemed Siemens unattractive. The cost of this inexperience, as an investor, was high. How high?

In 1970, a share of Philips was worth about $14; today it is worth about $23. The return on Philips to a U.S. investor amounted to about 2.5 percent per annum. Siemens, in contrast, was then worth about $43 per share and today is worth about $440 per share, or an average annual return of 12.3 percent per annum. For comparison, over the same period, the S&P 500 Composite Index rose from 90.3 to 353.8, for an average return of about 7.0 percent per year. So, had I been able to breach the wall of German accounting, I would have made a much more rewarding investment and also outperformed my own market—which is, after all, the sole purpose of foreign diversification. (Note: If dividends were included, Philips would look better, but still much poorer than Siemens.)

We all know what happened to Hadrian's Wall. It crumbled under the continuing forays of marauding Scotts, and the Romans eventually gave up on the British Isles and went back to the warmth and comfort of Rome. In an analytical sense, the walls of accounting secrecy are crumbling throughout Europe, but the onslaught is multifaceted and multinational—driven by analysts, portfolio counselors, private investors, stock exchange listing requirements, and, in Europe, the European Economic Community (EEC) regulations. In markets everywhere, investors are demanding to know: What do I own? What did my company earn? What are its assets worth? How has my management discharged its duties? How has my board of directors discharged its duties? And, in whose interest? Fortunately for investors, there is no pleasant home for publicly listed companies to return to. The international investor will not relent, and I predict that in the next 10 years the level of disclosure in Europe will at least match that of the United States and the United Kingdom today.

Global Investing in the Future

I have learned a lot during my 20 years of trial, error, and frustration. One of the most important considerations for the analyst of the future is to understand differences in accounting practices. **Table 1** summarizes the major accounting differences between the larger European countries and the United States. Although this is not adequate information for an accountant, I believe it does a reasonable job of highlighting the areas that call for in-depth analysis by the working security analyst.

The key areas of concern, all of which involve German, Swiss, and (although not included in Table 1) Italian accounting, relate to (1) the obfuscation of cash movements—the absence of any kind of cash-flow statement, or the absence of a reliable one; (2) the overstatement of costs and liabilities; and (3) the understatement of profits and assets. All of these countries also suffer from the lack of consolidation of significant majority and minority interests (foreign and domestic). The following are a few areas that cannot be taken at face value.

- Costs of goods sold are routinely overstated in West Germany.

Table 1. Major Accounting Differences: Europe and the United States

	Degree of Overall Conservatism	Depreciation	Revenue Recognition	Asset Valuation	Pension Accounting	Subsidiary Accounting	Loss Provisions	Tax Accounting	System of Accounting
United States	5	Generally SL or modified accelerated; very long asset lives	Shipment or POC	Historic less depreciation; market for securities	Fully accrued, generally vested and overfunded	Fully consolidated at 50%; single line 20-50%	As realized, no accrual	Accrual, generally large deferrals	Accrual
West Germany	2	Extremely rapid at management's discretion; very short asset lives	Shipment or completion	Lowest value principle	Large balance-sheet accruals, large off-balance-sheet reserves	Foreign subsidiaries consolidated at management's discretion; domestic over 50%; less than 50% dividends only	At management's discretion; large on- and off-balance-sheet provisions	Actual tax paid (i.e., cash), no on-balance-sheet accruals, sometimes large off-balance-sheet reserves	Cash
Switzerland	1	Same	Same	Same	Off-balance-sheet reserves, generally overfunded	For all but the largest multinationals (e.g., Nestle) no consolidation; dividends received only	Same—generally off-balance-sheet	Same	Cash
Holland	4	Rapid, short asset lives	Same	Historic less depreciation	Off-balance-sheet, fully funded and vested	Over 50% fully; 20-50% single line	As recognized	Fully accrued, large deferral accounts	Accrual
Belgium	3	Rapid, short asset lives, management discretion on "extra" depreciation	Same	Mixture of historic net and lowest value	Same	Same	Recognition	Fully accrued	Accrual
France	3	Same	Same	Same	Same	Same	Same	Same	Accrual
Sweden	6	Same	Same	Historic less depreciation	Same	Same	Same	Actual, no accrual	Accrual
United Kingdom	7	SL, long asset lives	Shipment or POC	Historic less depreciation except for fixed assets which are valued every three years generally upward. Also, no LIFO on inventories	Same	Same	Same	Same	Liberal accrual

- Consolidations are universally incomplete, often for controlled subsidiaries that are material, in West Germany, Switzerland, Spain, and Italy.
- The cost of pension, contingency, liability, and rainy-day provisions are all routinely and grossly overstated in West Germany, Switzerland, Spain, Italy, and, to a lesser but still significant degree, France and Holland. By contrast, they are optimistically provided for in the United Kingdom and parts of Scandinavia.
- The value of assets is universally and dramatically understated in West Germany and Switzerland because of the use of the lowest-value principle and the excessively rapid depreciation of physical assets. In Italy, France, and Spain, carrying values are routinely far below net market values because of the use of historical cost, rapid depreciation, and relatively high inflation rates. In Holland and Scandinavia, overly rapid depreciation understates values. Conversely, in the United Kingdom physical assets are routinely marked to market. For some U.K. companies, this revaluation of real physical assets often accounts for between 50 and 75 percent of the disclosed net worth.

Let me highlight some of the dramatic differences among the countries. For example, under asset valuation, West Germany uses the lowest value principle. That is an amusing term. To give one example, the Deutsche Bank is rumored to have written down its new headquarters in Frankfurt to one mark the day it was put into service, on the premise that it was a purpose-built facility with no tangible value to any other user. The actual cost of the building, which is quite elaborate, was probably over DM 1.0 billion. Another example is the Colonia Insurance Company, which spent DM 250 million to build a new headquarters outside of Cologne and wrote it down to DM 25 million on the day the staff walked in the door. That is a very dramatic difference, and the practice is most prevalent in West Germany and Switzerland.

Pension accounting is another area where there are significant differences. Outside of the Anglo-Saxon world, fully vested, fully funded, off-balance-sheet, trusteed pension funds are rare. Most companies have a gentlemen's agreement to pay pensions as long as they are able. There may be a legal liability, or there may be some preference as a creditor to pension beneficiaries, but pension liability is not funded and lodged with trustees.

The next area of difference is subsidiary accounting. In some countries, subsidiaries are consolidated when they are more than 50 percent owned, whereas in other countries management might decide it is inappropriate to consolidate. The first time I called on Nestle, in 1977, for example, the only revenues disclosed were from the Swiss operation, even though at that point about 95 percent of their operations were outside of Switzerland. In addition, companies do not always consolidate the same companies from year to year. Sometimes they consolidate companies that have a loss, because they do not want to show a large gain in earnings that year, and then other times they consolidate a company with a large profit because they have losses in other operations. The only way you can find out what they are doing is to ask them.

In the United States and the United Kingdom, losses are taken when they are realized—or at least when they are definite; there are no provisions for nonspecific loss accruals. In West Germany, Switzerland, Italy, and Spain, you can make all sorts of provisions for the sky falling or anything else you can think of, and in a number of these countries they are allowed by the tax authorities.

All of the foregoing means that some real digging is required to determine the true assets and earnings of companies in many European countries. This is not done as frequently as it should be, in my experience, which is a polite way of saying that it is rarely done.

Table 2 shows estimates of changes in asset values, earnings, and cash flow in the EEC countries relative to U.S. GAAP, with full provision for potential preferred tax liability, realistic economic depreciation of physical assets, and full accrual accounting principles employed. If West Germany went to a uniform system of accounting similar to the one in the United Kingdom, Holland, or the United States, I estimate cash flow would increase by 50 to 70 percent. In Italy, Spain, Switzerland, and, most prominently, West Germany, companies routinely disguise cash flow. They do this by simply making a provision in the income statement for a cost that does not exist. The money thus disappears from the balance sheet, and it does not show up in the cash-flow figures.

Table 2. Estimate of Changes in Relative Asset Values, Earnings, and Cash Flow

| | *Post-1992 in the EEC* | | |
	Assets	*Earnings*	*Cash Flow*
United Kingdom	Unchanged	−20-30%	Unchanged
France	+20-50%	+20-30%	+10-15%
Belgium	+20-50%	+20-30%	+10-15%
Holland	+10-25%	+10-15%	Unchanged
West Germany	+100%	+100-200%	+50-70%

Adventures in German Accounting

I will illustrate some of the peculiarities of German accounting using Siemens and Volkswagen. Although the comparisons are for the 1982-86 period, I think they are still valid today.

Table 3 shows a comparison of Siemens with three major U.S. and U.K. diversified electrical equipment companies over the five-year period 1982-86. It is notable that General Electric (GE), Westinghouse, and GEC show very similar financial characteristics. Siemens, on the other hand, differs in many categories from the average of the other three, even though all four companies are in approximately the same business. Siemens differs in predictable ways. In the categories where it is hard to muddy the waters, Siemens's statistics are similar to the average of the other three; for example,

Table 3. Comparison of Electrical Equipment Companies: Five-Year Average (1982-86)

	GE*	Westinghouse**	GEC, plc	Westinghouse GE, GEC plc Average	Siemens
Net income/cash flow	55%	63%	63%	60%	21.5%
Dividends/cash flow	26%	20%	21%	22%	8.8%
Cash flow/turnover	11%	10%	12%	11%	11.3%
Cash flow/assets	11%	13%	23%	16%	10.9%
Depreciation/cash flow	41%	36%	31%	36%	38.2%
Cap. expenditures/net cash flow	56%	43%	37%	45%	38.3%
Gross margins	17%	24%	22%	21%	17.4%
Pretax margins	9%	9%	13%	10%	5.4%
Net margins	6%	6%	8%	7%	2.4%
Market cap./book value	266%	244%	143%	218%	21.0%

*   Excludes GECC (revenues, pretax, and net income).
**   Excludes WCC, extraordinary items.
Note: 1986 calendar year for GE and WX, 3/31/87 fiscal year for GEC, 9/30/82-86 fiscal year for Siemens.

cash flow as a percentage of turnover, depreciation as a percentage of cash flow, and gross margin ratios.

Clearly, there are a number of things Siemens calls expenses that the rest of the world calls profits. Just to show you how understated its income statement is, in this five-year period Siemens had interest earnings of DM 11 billion and interest expenses of DM 4.6 billion, which were largely related to hedging operations, for net interest earned of DM 6.4 billion. The total declared pretax profit in this period was DM 12.5 billion, leading one to presume they only made DM 6.1 billion in profits over five years of operation on turnover of DM 227 billion—a 2.6 percent pretax margin. They also had an extremely high tax rate, so you can argue about what earnings really are. Clearly, what Siemens declares as profit is fictional—and very low.

To make Siemens comparable to U.S. companies, I restated their asset and equity values for the five-year period (see the calculations in **Table 4**). Throughout this period, Siemens never sold for more than 40 percent of true asset value, according to my calculations. Today, the stock is selling at DM 740, which is about 15 percent higher than the price of DM 646 when I did this study. There have been three additional years of asset appreciation and retained earnings, however, so I estimate Siemens is now selling at about 30 to 35 percent of true net asset value.

I have done a similar comparison of automobile manufacturers. **Table 5** presents a comparison of Volkswagen, Ford, General Motors, and Peugeot—I have aggregated the figures for 1984-86. Based on the gross margin, Volkswagen is more profitable than Ford and General Motors, and just a bit less profitable than Peugeot. At the net-income level, the comparison is less favorable. To me, it is clear that Volkswagen's stated net income is not comparable. For example, Volkswagen had a tax rate of 86.2 percent, but its cash flow was about 12 percent of revenues over this period; Ford's was 11 percent and General Motors's was 12 percent, which would lead you to

Table 4.   Restatement of Siemens's Assets and Equity (DM billions)

	1982	1983	1984	1985	1986	Five-Year Average
Dividends paid	328	351	442	573	576	
Dividends/cash flow	8.0%	7.4%	9.2%	9.9%	9.5%	8.8%
Net income/cash flow	17.9%	17.0%	22.1%	26.3%	24.4%	21.5%
Capital expenditures/ net fixed assets	28.6%	27.6%	37.1%	51.9%	37.7%	36.6%
Depreciations/net fixed assets	23.8%	25.4%	26.4%	26.3%	22.4%	24.9%
Miscellaneous expenditures	7,598.2	7,430.8	8,982.8	11,448.3	9,328.6	N/A
Misc. expenditures/ turnover	18.9%	18.8%	19.6%	21.0%	19.8%	19.6%
Misc. expenditures/ COGS	23.8%	22.6%	23.9%	27.9%	21.4%	23.9%
Misc. expenditures/ net fixed assets	122.7%	120.9%	137.5%	142.8%	72.8%	119.3%
Year-end debt (8)	6,698.7	6,711.2	6,502.9	6,610.2	8,251.5	
Average debt (8)	N/A	6,705.0	6,607.1	6,556.6	7,404.1	
Implied average cost of debt	13.7%	12.5%	15.3%	15.2%	10.6%	
Marketable securities: Equities	264.1	461.6	610.6	807.2	1,259.1	
Interest-bearing securities	5,186.5	8,155.7	11,458.0	11,844.4	13,520.2	
Unlisted loan notes	4,237.5	5,635.5	6,127.4	6,672.7	5,842.9	
Cash & equivalents	1,427.7	2,298.5	1,290.1	1,215.8	1,268.2	
Liquid assets at carrying value	11,115.4	16,551.3	19,486.1	20,540.2	21,890.4	
Excess of market value of securities over carrying value	9,415.4	17,504.5	25,137.1	36,350.7	39,900.4	
Declared equity	9,980.0	10,824.4	11,648.5	13,266.7	15,134.2	
Provisions-pensions	5,483.7	6,751.9	7,744.8	8,792.3	9,329.1	
Miscellaneous	8,527.4	9,492.3	11,776.2	14,192.1	14,520.4	
Total equity equivalent	33,406.3	44,573.1	56,306.6	72,601.9	78,884.1	
Total assets	36,781.7	40,441.0	47,206.9	52,140.9	58,331.5	
Cash flow/assets	11.2%	11.7%	10.2%	11.1%	10.4%	10.9%
Net income/assets	2.0%	2.0%	2.3%	2.9%	2.5%	2.3%
Market capitalization	10,193	15,277	19,184	28,724	31,999	16,560
Market capitalization/ true equity	31%	34%	34%	40%	40%	21%

believe that Volkswagen was just as profitable as either Ford or General Motors—until you looked at the net profit line.

   Table 6 presents Volkswagen's restated assets and equity, according to my calculations. The results are similar to those for Siemens. In February 1988, Volkswagen was selling for a little more than 4 percent of sales, Ford was about 14 percent, and General Motors was about 8 percent. Another interesting thing about Volkswagen is that over this five-year period they had DM 6.4 billion in interest income net of interest expense, and DM 6.4 billion in pretax income, which would lead you to believe they were running the car division as a hobby.

Table 5. Comparison of Automobile Manufacturers (1984-86 Aggregates)

	VW	(A) Ford	(B) GM	(C) Peugeot[a]	(A+B+C) Aggregate	VW[b]
Sales	DM 151,146	$167,857	$280,475	$51,972	= $500,304	$89,327
COGS	127,956	147,386	252,914	42,586	= 442,886	75,622
Gross margin[c]	15.4%	12.2%	9.8%	18.0%	= 11.5%	15.4%
Taxes paid	4,613	4,206	3,135	214	= 7,555	2,726
Tax rate	86.2%	32.6%	21.4%	35.0%	= 26.8%	76.7%
Net income	1,404	8,707	11,505	397	= 20,609	830
Dividend rate	666	1,404	4,804	0	= 6,208	394
Interest earned	4,282	2,345	3,609	225	= 6,179	2,531
Cash flow	17,351	18,438	33,345	2,561	= 54,344	10,254
Depreciation	10,286	7,661	17,771	2,169	= 27,601	6,079
Capital expenditures	12,536	10,605	17,780	2,316	= 30,701	7,409
Market cap. 2/10/88	DM 6,324	$ 23,351	$ 21,413	$ 3,582	= $ 48,346	$ 3,737

[a] Shown in U.S. dollars (FF = $0.175).
[b] Shown in U.S. dollars (DM = $0.591).
[c] Gross margin is reciprocal of the sum of materials, wages, compulsory Social Security contributions, purchased materials and services, pension contributions (Ford, GM, and Peugeot), and depreciation, divided by sales.

Source: Capital Research Company, based on company annual reports.

Using the same analysis of net asset value as we used in Siemens, you can see that Volkswagen did not sell for more than 26 percent of estimated net asset value during this five-year period. Since that time, Volkswagen has risen about 60 percent to DM 550, but there have been almost three additional years of profits and asset appreciation, so I think it is still selling for only about 30 percent of net asset value.

Clearly, there is a need to better understand accounting standards around the world, particularly in West Germany.

Conclusion

There are many undervalued companies in Europe. There are still undervalued companies in West Germany, despite the rapid rise of the West German market in the three months ending January 31, 1990. The extent of undervaluation is just as great in Switzerland, although it is primarily related to the lack of consolidation. Italy has shown very little gain and is the least expensive market in the world on a price-to-cash-earnings basis. Holland, the second-best-performing market in Europe over the past 20 years and the fourth-best-performing market in the world over the same period, is the second-cheapest market in the world, selling at about five times cash earnings.

In contrast, the three markets on which analysts seem to spend the most time—the United States, United Kingdom, and Japan—offer very little relative attraction on a valuation basis. The markets in the United States and the United Kingdom have had rather mediocre performance over the past 20 years.

My conclusion is that foreign markets in general, and European markets in particular, are a veritable paradise for fundamental analysts. Forget the

Table 6.   Restatement of Volkswagen's Assets and Equity (DM billions)

	1982	1983	1984	1985	1986	Five-Year Average
Dividends paid	0	0	120	240	306	N/A
Dividends/cash flow	0	0	2.4%	3.8%	5.0%	2.2%
Net income/cash flow	0	0	4.6%	9.4%	9.5%	3.6%
Cap. expenditures/ net fixed assets	43.0%	41.0%	31.0%	39.0%	61.0%	43.0%
Depreciations/net fixed assets	26.0%	29.0%	44.0%	39.0%	28.0%	33.0%
Misc. expenditures	4,507	4,440	5,863	7,280	7,758	N/A
Misc. expenditures/ turnover	12.0%	11.0%	13.0%	14.0%	15.0%	13.0%
Misc. expenditures/ COGS	13.0%	12.0%	15.0%	17.0%	18.0%	15.0%
Misc. expenditures/ net fixed assets	39.0%	38.0%	65.0%	83.0%	74.0%	60.0%
Year-end debt	5,895	6,657	7,517	6,712	7,484	
Average debt	N/A	6,276	7,087	7,114	7,098	
Implied average cost of debt	24.1%	23.1%	20.6%	20.4%	15.9%	
Marketable securities at carrying value	3,062	4,636	4,326	6,379	3,240	
Cash & equivalents	1,952	1,815	5,253	4,326	9,510	
Liquid assets at carrying value	5,014	6,451	9,579	10,723	12,750	
Excess of market value of securities over carrying value	10,407	10,267	16,705	23,676	26,368	
Declared equity	6,334	6,708	6,685	7,395	10,482	
Provisions-pensions	3,626	4,235	4,739	5,029	5,279	
Miscellaneous	4,570	5,579	7,417	9,343	9,387	
Total equity equivalent	24,937	26,807	35,546	45,443	51,518	
Total assets	25,893	28,755	32,942	34,822	40,709	
Cash flow/assets	12.7%	14.2%	15.0%	18.1%	14.9%	2/9/99
Net income/assets	N/A	N/A	0.7%	1.8%	1.4%	
Market capitalization	3,504	5,256	4,896	11,808	12,606	6,210
Market capitalization/ true equity (12/31)	14.0%	20.0%	14.0%	26.0%	24.0%	12.0%

Source: Author's estimates, based on company reports.

economic forecasts and the central bank policy. Look at the companies and understand what they offer. If you do, I think you will agree that we are, at most, halfway there in the process of truly appreciating the great values that exist in many foreign companies.

Quantitative Techniques for Portfolio Management, Part I

William E. Jacques, CFA
Partner and Chief Investment Officer
Martingale Asset Management

My firm is a domestic U.S. equity manager; international equities are my hobby. Increasingly, we have found that we must have a global perspective to manage stocks in the United States. There are influences affecting U.S. stock prices that we cannot understand from a U.S. perspective. We have to know what influences are entering the marketplace, who the marginal investor is, and how to value stocks. Even though we are a U.S.-only investment manager, we have adopted a global perspective to stock valuation.

One of the most important issues in international investing is whether the global markets are integrated or segmented. If the global markets are integrated, one may use the same approach to investing in all countries. With unrestricted capital movement, capital will flow to the economy that has the highest expected returns. Stock prices will be set by the global investor. On the other hand, if there are barriers to the free flow of capital, there will be differences in the way companies are valued from one country to the next. Analysts will have to come up with country- or industry-specific valuation models. For example, should one approach analysis on a country-by-country basis or with a global industry perspective? Should the analyst look at Japanese stocks or at the global automobile industry? Analysts will also have to determine whether fundamental valuation factors are equally important in all countries. For example, is firm size related to price to the same degree in the United Kingdom as it is in the United States?

I will address these issues in this presentation. I will also present my theory about why there are differences across borders and industries, something we call the law of the marginal investor—an investor who, wherever he happens to be, drives stock prices.

Country Versus Industry Analysis

The consensus seems to be that markets are not totally integrated; they are segmented enough to make a difference. To have an integrated market you must have a rapid flow of capital around the world and not have political risks, trade restrictions, or differences between countries in taxes, transaction costs, and local taste and preferences. People all over the world would have to like the same things. The world is not like this, so we believe it is necessary to take the differences into consideration.

In 1988 we examined whether there were differences in company valuations across industries and countries. We considered three levels of differences: global industry, country, and industry within country. The study covered companies in Japan, the United Kingdom, and the United States. We used price/earnings (P/E) ratios to determine the degree of comparability. Price and earnings-per-share data as of December 1987 were obtained from the Morgan Stanley Capital International Perspective database. There were 20 companies in each of 6 industries in each of 3 countries, for a total of 360 companies.

Table 1 shows the P/E ratios of all 360 companies grouped by country. As you might expect, the P/E multiple in Japan (41) was significantly different than that in the United States (11.2) or the United Kingdom (11.8). The difference between the Japanese and U.S. valuations was so large that, statistically, there was only one chance in a million that the same phenomenon was taking place in all three countries. This could mean either that the valuation per unit of earnings is much higher in Japan or that the earnings are on a different basis. Either way, there is a significant difference in valuation, based on P/E, across the three countries.

Table 1. Do Countries Matter?

	December 1987 Price/Earnings	Number of Companies
Japan	41.0	120
United States	11.2	120
United Kingdom	11.8	120

Next, we grouped all companies by industry to see if there is a global industry effect. Each of the 6 global industry groups contained 60 companies. Again, we used the P/E multiples by industry to compare the companies within the industries. **Table 2** shows that the low relative valuation of finance companies is a global phenomenon. Companies in the finance industry have the lowest P/E multiple, whereas the service companies, on a worldwide basis, have a significantly higher P/E multiple. We concluded that global industries are important, and analysts should take them into consideration.

Table 2. Do Global Industries Matter?

	December 1987 Price/Earnings	Number of Companies
Finance	11.8	60
Materials	14.1	60
Energy	14.4	60
Consumer goods	16.7	60
Capital equipment	17.6	60
Services	18.2	60
	Total	360

In the third part of the study we grouped companies by both country and industry. **Table 3** shows these results. There is evidence of an interaction between countries and industries. For example, the capital equipment industry in Japan has a P/E multiple that is above the Japanese average, but in the United Kingdom the capital equipment industry has a P/E multiple of 10.1, which is below the U.K. average. Also, the P/E multiple of energy in Japan was 23.6, well below average, whereas the energy sector in the United Kingdom had a P/E multiple of 16.3, which was well above average. Hence, the proper comparison group for a company looks to be more than just its country average or global industry average, but the average of companies in the same country and industry.

Table 3.   Do Industries Within Countries Matter?

	December 1987 Price/Earnings			
	Japan	*United States*	*United Kingdom*	*Average*
Finance	39.8	7.3	11.0	11.8
Materials	45.5	11.1	9.9	14.1
Energy	23.6	9.5	16.3	14.4
Consumer goods	50.0	13.1	12.0	16.7
Capital equipment	56.8	18.6	10.1	17.6
Services	52.1	13.7	13.8	18.2
Average	41.0	11.2	11.8	15.1

We used a two-way analysis of variance test to determine which of the three effects is the strongest. The results indicate that all three of the effects are statistically significant at the 0.0001 level—there is only one chance out of 10,000 that the differences observed could have occurred by chance. Country differences are the most important effect—what is happening in Japan is different from what is happening in the United Kingdom or the United States. The industry within a country is the next most important effect—the fact that you have a capital goods company in Japan or the United Kingdom is very important. Global industries are the least important effect.

Valuation Factors Across Countries

The first part of our study concluded that company valuations differ across countries and that industries are important as well. The second part of our study examined whether there were other valuation factors that were important. For instance, it is generally believed that investors in Japan are very concerned with company size. One would expect prices and valuations to be positively influenced by company size in Japan (bigger is better). Is that also true in the United States or the United Kingdom?

In 1988 we examined valuation factors across countries. We examined whether it is appropriate to use the same stock valuation model across all countries, or whether it may be better to build individual valuation models for each country. Theory suggests that if international capital markets are completely integrated, then an equilibrium model, such as a dividend discount model, would be suitable. If markets are completely segregated, a different model for each country would be better.

We related stock prices to current earnings per share, current dividends per share, forecast earnings per share, growth in earnings, book value, beta, and size. All data except the growth in earnings data were obtained from Morgan Stanley Capital International Perspective PC database; the earnings-growth data were derived from Lynch, Jones and Ryan's I/B/E/S International Edition. We observed both pre-crash (September 1987) and post-crash (December 1987) periods to determine how the crash might have affected differential valuations across countries.

We used a cross-sectional regression to identify the level of importance of each of the factors in determining stock prices in the United States, Japan, and the United Kingdom. The general form of the model is:

$$\text{PRICE}_{ict} = \alpha_{1ct}\text{VAR1}_{ict} + \alpha_{2ct}\text{VAR2}_{ict} + \ldots + \alpha_{nct}\text{VARN}_{ict},$$

where $VARN$ = fundamental variable N (e.g., MSE or DIVPS), α_{nct} = coefficient on variable N for country c and time period t, and PRICE_{ict} = price of stock i in country c at time period t.

We used the t-statistic as the measure of the relative importance of each factor. One must be careful in the interpretation of t-statistics, however. For instance, current earnings may prove to be statistically significant in one country but not in another. Investors may truly value the economic earnings in the second country, but the accounting earnings that are reported in that country may be randomly related to economic earnings and, hence, the model would not pick up on the relation. For now, we will assume that accounting earnings are equally representative of economic earnings across countries.

If investors do not care about current earnings, there will be no correlation between earnings and prices. **Table 4** shows that current earnings are important to investors in Japan, the United Kingdom, and the United States. Current earnings became somewhat more important after the October 1987 crash than before, as illustrated by the statistics for December 1987 versus September 1987. The R^2 statistic indicates that 75 percent of the differences in stock prices in the United Kingdom are explained by only one variable—current earnings. In the United States, current earnings explained about 50 percent of the differences in stock prices, and in Japan they explained 61

Table 4. Importance of Current Earnings

	Japan	United Kingdom	United States
September 1987			
Coefficient	32.40	14.50	12.80
t-statistic	19.50	22.80	17.60
R^2	0.61	0.75	0.50
December 1987			
Coefficient	31.60	9.60	9.90
t-statistic	24.90	23.60	21.40
R^2	0.71	0.76	0.57

percent. Based on these results, we concluded that a very simple model of relating stock prices to current earnings works very well in all three countries.

We also tested the model of price as a function of dividends, and compared the results to the model of price as a function of earnings. **Table 5** shows the relative importance of current earnings versus current dividends. Investors in these countries seem to place more importance on earnings than on dividends. This is particularly true in the United States. Dividends seem to matter the most to the U.K. investors. In Japan, the P/E model is about twice as good as the dividend/earnings model. In the United Kingdom, it did not matter which model was used, perhaps because the dividend policy there is a direct function of earnings. In the United States, the P/E model is much more valuable than the price/dividend model; in fact, prices relate fairly well to earnings but not at all to dividends, which contrasts sharply with results for the United Kingdom.

Table 5. Current Earnings Versus Dividends

	Japan		United Kingdom		United States	
	Earnings	*Dividends*	*Earnings*	*Dividends*	*Earnings*	*Dividends*
September 1987						
Coefficient	32.40	110.50	14.50	23.80	12.80	14.00
t-statistic	19.50	11.20	22.80	17.50	17.60	5.30
R^2	0.61	0.33	0.75	0.65	0.50	0.08
December 1987						
Coefficient	31.60	122.90	9.60	17.20	9.90	12.20
t-statistic	24.90	14.70	23.60	22.00	21.40	7.20
R^2	0.71	0.45	0.76	0.74	0.57	0.13

The strength of the P/E model makes me question why people do not use earnings discount models instead of dividend discount models. Clearly, in many of these countries, the statistical strength of the earnings model is stronger than the dividend model.

The next step in the analysis was to look at the relation between prices and forecast earnings. **Table 6** shows the relative importance of current earnings versus forecast earnings. Across the board, forecast earnings are more closely related to stock prices than current earnings. This is most noticeable in the United States. Our analysis shows that forecasted earnings did relate better to stock prices and that they did explain more of stock price differences than did the historical earnings.

Table 6. Current Versus Forecast Earnings

	Japan		United Kingdom		United States	
	Current	*Forecast*	*Current*	*Forecast*	*Current*	*Forecast*
September 1987						
Coefficient	32.40	31.20	14.50	11.50	12.80	13.00
t-statistic	19.50	25.50	22.80	25.10	17.60	28.30
R^2	0.61	0.72	0.75	0.79	0.50	0.72
December 1987						
Coefficient	31.60	29.90	9.60	8.50	9.90	11.00
t-statistic	24.90	31.50	23.60	27.60	21.40	36.50
R^2	0.71	0.79	0.76	0.82	0.57	0.79

Table 7 shows the results of our multiple-factor valuation model. The multiple-factor framework lets us examine the relationship between stock prices and each factor, net of all the other factors. It shows that current earnings are important to investors in all three countries. Thus, P/E-based models should work well in all three countries. Company size is quite significant for stock prices in the United States and Japan. Forecast earnings growth is important to U.K. investors and not as important to either U.S. or Japanese investors. Current dividends are only important to U.K. investors. Thus, one might question the value of a dividend discount model in the United States or Japan.

Table 7. Valuation Factors Ranked by Country

	Japan		*United Kingdom*		*United States*	
	9/87	*12/87*	*9/87*	*12/87*	*9/87*	*12/87*
Current earnings	1	1	1	1	2	2
Dividends per share	5–	6–	3	2	4–	5
Growth in earnings	4	4	2	3	6	6
Beta	6	5	6–	5–	5–	4–
Book value	2	3	5–	6–	3	3
Size	3	2	4	4	1	1
N	249	260	165	172	311	351

Note: The negative after the number means the sign was the opposite of what was expected (e.g., for September 1987, price was negatively related to dividends in Japan, net of other factors).

With regard to the other factors, growth seems to have been more important to U.K. and Japanese investors than to the U.S. investors. Beta appeared irrelevant to pricing. Beta may be a good risk measure in portfolio constructions, but perhaps less relevant to investors on a stock-by-stock basis. Investors did not seem to care what the beta was in any country in the pricing of stocks. Book value is important to both Japanese and U.S. investors, but not that important to U.K. investors, which is surprising. It is important to Japanese investors despite the fact that book values are dramatically understated in Japan.

Other things being equal, there is no reason why the P/E ratio of a big company should be higher or lower than the P/E ratio of a small company. In fact, size was the single most important determinant of prices in the United States. Big companies had higher P/E ratios than small companies. Company size is important to Japanese investors, but it does not seem to be important in the United Kingdom.

Conclusion

It appears that different valuation factors seem to be important in each country. There appear to be enough differences for us to adopt an investment strategy that is based on segmented markets, but beware of the marginal investor and his effect on pricing. If the Japanese investor becomes the marginal investor in the United Kingdom, then perhaps the valuation factors that are important to investors in Japan will become more important to the pricing of U.K. stocks.

Quantitative Techniques for Portfolio Management, Part II

Andrew Rudd
President and Chief Executive Officer
BARRA

People are beginning to apply quantitative techniques used in the United States to other markets. The big question is whether the factors that influence security prices domestically are the same as the factors that influence security prices globally. In this presentation, I will discuss some of my findings.

One of the amusing things about the application of quantitative analysis to the global markets over the past few years has been the development of a folklore as to how global investing works. The folklore goes something like this:

- The world is a single financial market;
- The world is becoming more global and integrated;
- There is a small-stock effect globally;
- Dividend discount models do not work in Japan, which is overvalued;
- The international data are so bad that quantitative models do not work;
- Country timing is an easy strategy;
- Currencies do not matter;
- Country allocation is the most important decision; and
- Global bonds are not a proper asset class.

All of these issues are interesting, and all can be analyzed objectively using quantitative analysis.

The Quantitative Approach

The quantitative approach to investing provides a framework for addressing many of the issues involved in global investing. **Figure 1** outlines the important processes that make up a quantitative approach: the information process, portfolio construction, and implementation and monitoring.

The information process is the process of transforming data—financial, demographic, earnings, and so on—into refined information. Portfolio managers and analysts use the refined information as a signal to differentiate undervalued assets from overvalued assets; it is the alpha in quantitative terms. For most managers around the world, this process is unspecified and untested. It turns out, however, that one can develop a very systematic information process. Although this is the most exciting process, it is the one most frequently neglected, and the one least understood by practitioners.

The portfolio construction process is the process of transforming the refined information into an optimal portfolio and a trade list. It involves combining the alphas with information on the investor—his goals, constraints, benchmarks, and so forth—and with an assessment of the manager's

Figure 1. The Quantitative Approach

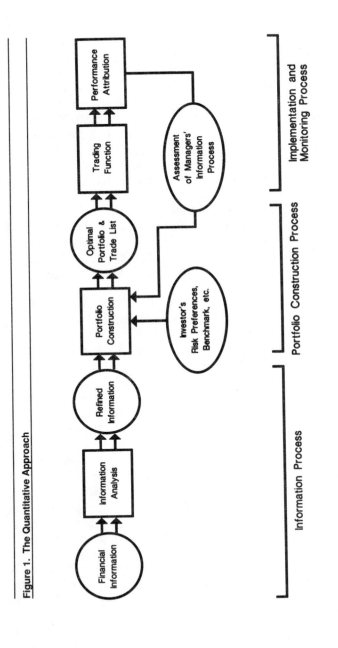

Source: Rudd, Andrew. "Fixed Income Management." In C. Stoakes and A. Freeman, eds. *Managing Global Portfolios.* London: Euromoney Publications.

information process to determine an optimal portfolio. Most people think of this aspect of the process as the black box. To make the black box work, one must specify the risk model—the relative risks of the assets under consideration. The quality of the risk model is crucial to the efficiency with which one can obtain the optimal portfolios.

The implementation and monitoring process comprises the trading function and performance attribution. In the international markets, implementation is very important because the cost of trading is relatively high. The performance attribution process is equally important; the process depends on understanding how the performance was derived. Is the performance the result of choosing the right countries? The right industries? The right stocks? Or the right currencies? The performance attribution analysis provides feedback, which enables us to assess the manager's information process. It verifies the information analysis in the beginning, and it tells us whether things have changed. For example, is the yen-dollar relation more volatile now than it was earlier? The trading function is related to this feedback loop, because you may want to implement different trading strategies in different environments.

Most people think that quantitative approaches involve only the specification of an optimal portfolio. This is, however, only part of the process. If one overlooks the importance of the information process, the definition of the risk model, or the implementation and monitoring, one misses a large part of what a systematic approach can do for you.

The Modeling Process

Integral to the portfolio construction process is the identification of a risk model. It turns out that the risk model also underlies the portfolio performance attribution process, the trading function, and the information analysis process. So the identification of a risk model helps us to understand the relative movements of the assets that are coming in and most efficiently capture this in the portfolio.

The risk modeling process involves two phases. The first phase is to identify the characteristics of an asset that are associated with differences of return (i.e., size, price, price/earnings ratios, and so on). In a global investing setting, we are interested in whether otherwise-similar stocks that are domiciled in different countries perform differently. If so, one of those distinguishing characteristics should be the domicile. Another one should be the stock's industry. Other characteristics include capitalization, price volatility, and momentum. Typically, a measure of momentum is an important characteristic in local markets, and it would be interesting to see whether it is a characteristic common across markets.

The second phase is to estimate the returns associated with the identified characteristics. Typically, this is done by regressing the return on stocks against the identified characteristics. The returns associated with those characteristics may then be estimated.

Alternatively, for those of you who do not like regression, there is a portfolio management way to identify the returns to these characteristics:

construct a portfolio that is exposed only to the characteristic of interest. For example, if we want to find out what the pure return is to Japan, we would form a portfolio of Japanese stocks that is independent of other factors. Using the Morgan Stanley universe, the first step would be to buy only Japanese stocks (a 100 percent weighting in Japan and zero percent in the other countries). To eliminate exposure to industry returns, the holdings of the portfolio must be rearranged so that the industry exposure nets out to zero. This is accomplished with a combination of long and short positions. One would take similar actions to neutralize exposure to other factors, such as size. The result is a portfolio that is strange in its makeup, but that has one characteristic, Japan, and zero exposure everywhere else. This portfolio does not contain any money, either, because the long and short positions offset each other.

The performance of this portfolio over a month is the return to a pure Japan factor—uninfluenced, untarnished, perhaps even untainted—a natural expression of the pure Japanese effect. This process may be repeated for all of the factors affecting return, resulting in a series of returns, each of which is pure and is net of all the other effects.

The time series of factor returns indicates the sources of risk, how much they change through time, and the potential for misvaluation, enabling us to identify the effects that influence stock returns around the world. If the Japan return or the precious metal return is zero for the past five years, we would know that whatever return is picked up by an index of Japan or an index of pure metal is spurious, an artifact of some other influence. Or, if the time series of the pure Japan factor is constantly increasing through time, we are alerted to the fact that Japan may be overvalued.

Factor Returns

The quantitative approach methodology allows us to answer a lot of questions, including those raised by folklore. I will review the results of some of our research into factor returns.

Country Factors

Countries do have different return patterns. I will illustrate the country-return patterns for France, West Germany, Austria, and Japan. **Figure 2** shows the cumulative logarithmic return to France through the end of January 1990. I have plotted both the pure factor return and the index return, in this case the French subindex of the Financial Times Actuaries World Index. The pure return to France has approximately the same shape as the index return. The correlation between these two series gives us a measure of how integrated or segmented the French market is. It also tells us that the difference between these two series is the return, which is normally attributed to France, but which should be attributed to other characteristics because it is not purely French. In fact, it is due to global influences on the French market. The pure return to France has increased over most of this period.

Figure 3 shows the pure return to West Germany relative to an index of West German stocks. Because Germany has been in the news a lot recently, German stocks—and the index—have been influenced more by global

Figure 2. France: Cumulative Logarithmic Return

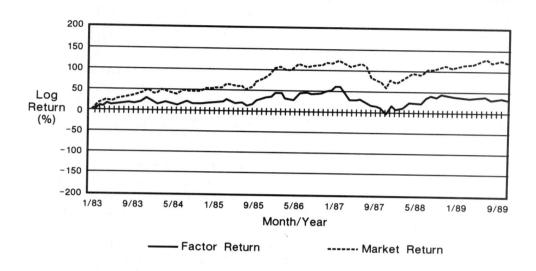

Source: BARRA

Figure 3. West Germany: Cumulative Logarithmic Return

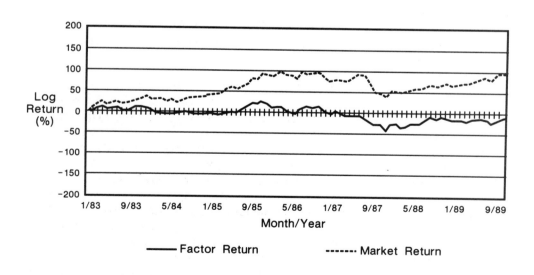

Source: BARRA

factors than by the pure German factor. Since the end of September 1989, there has been a strong German factor, net of other influences.

Figure 4 shows the pure return to Austria relative to an index of Austrian stocks. In Austria we see an even greater return that is pure Austria rather than the result of global effects.

Figure 5 shows the pure return to Japan relative to an index of Japanese stocks. This figure is quite interesting because it shows that there was a significant increase in the return to Japan starting around the end of 1985, when we had the price/earnings (P/E) explosion. It has dropped off again since the beginning of 1987. In fact, since January 1989, changes in the index of Japanese stocks were caused by global influences on Japan rather than a pure Japanese effect.

Global Size Factor

Research in the United States indicates that there is a return to size. The definition of a large company is straightforward within a country. It is more complicated on a global basis. We define size in terms of relative capitalization within a country rather than relative to the largest company in the world.

Our research shows that there is a global size factor. **Figure 6** shows the pure return to large companies, net of countries and net of other influences. As you can see, the return to large companies decreased from January 1983 to the beginning of 1989, meaning that large companies underperformed and small companies outperformed. Small companies globally showed a positive return net of other influences. More recently, however, there has been

---

Figure 4. Austria: Cumulative Logarithmic Return

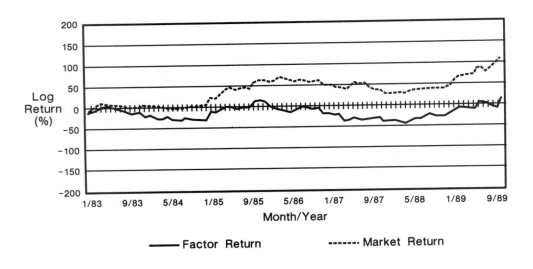

Source: BARRA

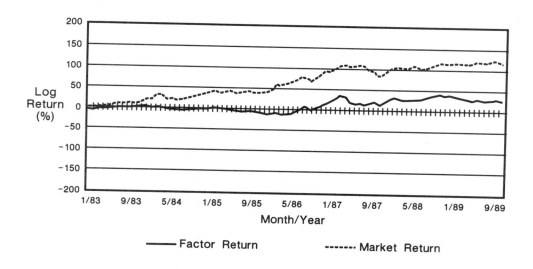

Figure 5. Japan: Cumulative Logarithmic Return

——— Factor Return   ------- Market Return

Source: BARRA

no size effect whatsoever. Small and large companies have performed relatively similarly, net of other influences.

Global Yield Factor

Our research shows that there is a global yield factor. **Figure 7** shows the pure return to yield. There is evidence of a positive yield factor up until January 1989. The logarithmic return would have been about 10 percent over that period, a little more than 1.5 percent per year for a pretty significant exposure to high-yielding stocks globally.[1]

Extensions of the Approach

This approach may be used to analyze the effect on returns of a more integrated Europe. For example, if you believe that the markets will become more integrated, you would expect that the industries will become more important than the countries, because to some extent, the country influence would be subsumed into a regional influence. This hypothesis may be tested by looking at the statistical significance of the country coefficients relative to the industry coefficients. This has not happened yet. The politicians may have been quite enamored of political integration, but the financial markets certainly do not reflect that interest.

---

[1]The significance of the global factors is discussed in more detail in an article by Grinbold, Rudd, and Stefek in the *Journal of Portfolio Management*, Fall 1989, pp. 79-88.

Figure 6: Size: Cumulative Logarithmic Returns

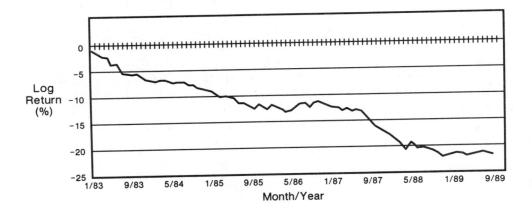

Source: BARRA

Figure 7: Yield: Cumulative Logarithmic Returns

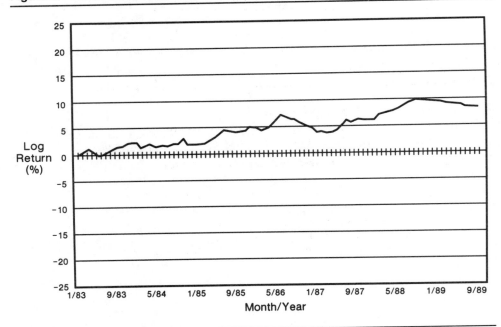

Source: BARRA

The Quantitative Approach to Bonds

The quantitative approach may be applied to the fixed-income market as well. In the analysis of fixed-income securities, the goal is to identify bond characteristics that are sources of return, for example the coupon, maturity, and payment frequency of a bond. **Figure 8** illustrates the fixed-income process.

There are several ways to approach the analysis of fixed-income returns. The approach that I favor is to develop both a currency risk model and a local country risk model. When these models are combined, it is possible to determine whether the factors that influence asset returns in one country will be the same factors that influence them in another country. For example, one can determine whether duration works as well in Switzerland as it does in

Figure 8: Fixed-Income Process

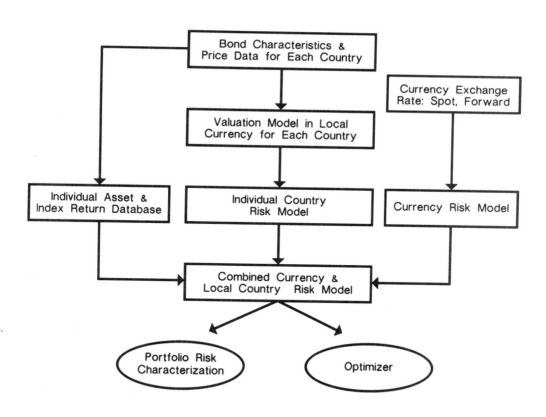

Source: BARRA

the United States or Japan. Using this approach, one can see very major differences in the characteristics of bond markets around the world.

Changes in the term structure are a source of return. I use a statistical technique called principal components analysis, which identifies the typical movement of the term structure in each of these markets. In theory, the term structure is supposed to make parallel shifts. To see whether this is in fact happening, one can compare the change in price for bonds at all maturities to the change in price for 30-year bonds in response to a 1-percent move. In reality, the term structure does not make parallel shifts, and a 1-percent move will result in a slightly different shape at the short end. The volatility is not constant across all maturities. **Figure 9** illustrates the first principal component for the United States, showing that the five- to ten-year rates move much more than the longer rates.

Figures 10 through 12 illustrate this factor for Japan, the United Kingdom, and West Germany, respectively. In Japan, for example, the long end of the term structure is the most variable, with relatively less volatility in the middle of the term structure. In the United Kingdom, relative to a 1-percent move in the 30-year bond benchmark, there is enormous volatility at the short end of the term structure, sometimes up to two times as much. The pattern in West Germany is very similar to the pattern in Japan, where the long-maturity bond is the most volatile, and one sees much less volatility in the mid-periods.

Figure 9. First Principal Component for United States*

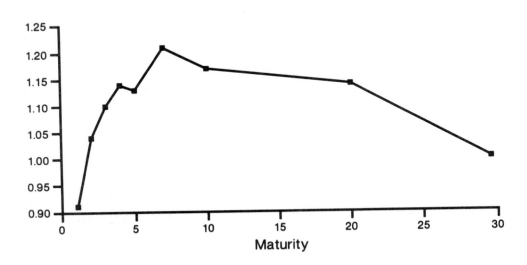

*Normalized to 1 percent at 30-year vertex.

Source: BARRA

Figure 10. First Principal Component for Japan*

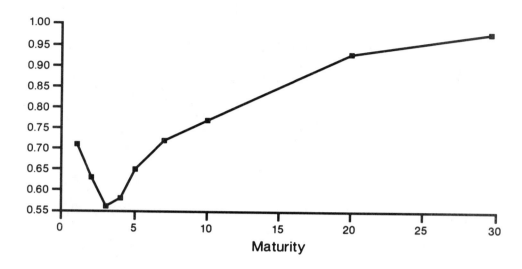

* Normalized to 1 percent at 30-year vertex.

Source: BARRA

Figure 11. First Principal Component for United Kingdom*

*Normalized to 1 percent at 30-year vertex

Source: BARRA

Figure 12. First Principal Component for West Germany*

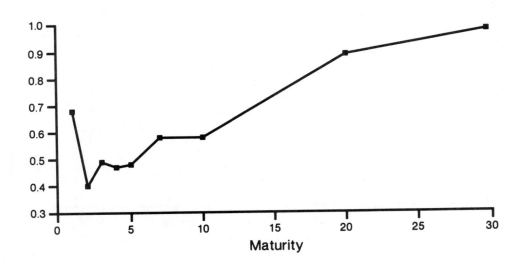

* Normalized to 1 percent at 30-year vertex.

Source: BARRA

Conclusion

I hope this has given you a flavor for multiple-factor risk modeling and how the identification of these returns can lead to a better understanding of the risk of portfolios, as well as provided some insight into the relative valuations of different characteristics in the market.

What Went Wrong with Perestroika?

Marshall Goldman

Associate Director
Russian Research Center, Harvard University
Kathryn Wasserman Davis Professor of Soviet Economics
Wellesley College

I am going to discuss the Soviet Union and Eastern Europe, and I should warn you that my comments are going to be very depressing.

These are incredible times. Around the world, communism is losing its grip at an awesome rate. The changes taking place in the Soviet Union and Eastern Europe are of such magnitude, and have taken place so swiftly, that it is difficult for us to remember that a few years ago our main concern regarding the U.S.S.R. had to do with the nuclear threat they posed. The Soviets were worried that the United States would strike first, and we were worried that they would strike first. These days, however, the political and economic status of the Soviet Union is our primary concern.

I must confess that I never thought I would see the Berlin Wall come down; that Eastern Europe from the Baltic to the Mediterranean would give up communism; that the Communist Party would no longer be a monopoly in some countries; or that the Communist Party would disappear altogether in others.

The same thing should be going on in the Soviet Union, but instead, the country has become mired in problems of its own making. Perestroika (economic reform) was heralded as a bold, innovative plan that would transport the Soviet economic system into a global market economy. Despite the intentions of Glasnost—the "openness" that has been viewed as so remarkable after years of operating under a shroud of secrecy and unflinching adherence to hard-line communist policies—the bright promise of a new era in the Soviet Union is fading.

The world has been watching the Soviet Union's steps toward a market economy, a more parliamentary political system, and an involvement in arms control; some of the results of these efforts have been remarkable. It is clear, however, that for every step taken toward these goals, the country has stumbled back in the face of continual problems that have prevented—and if not resolved soon, probably will continue to prevent—achievement of the goals that will have far-reaching effects around the world.

At the center of the storm is Mikhail Gorbachev, named by *Time* magazine as the "man of the decade." As far as I am concerned, he could be the man of the *century*, because there is no doubt in my mind that all of these changes would not have happened without him. He is deserving of the Nobel Prize.

At the same time, however, there is also a nightmarish side to developments in the Soviet Union. For the most part, those of us in the West have concentrated on what Gorbachev is doing in the areas that affect us. We have not seen beneath the surface. Not until recently have we learned what is really happening inside the economy. When I arrived at the airport in Moscow during a visit last month, I was greeted by my host, the Soviet deputy director of the Diplomatic Academy, which is their foreign service training organization underneath the Ministry of Foreign Affairs. My host greeted me and said, "Hello. My name is Ivan. Welcome to the Soviet Union. Welcome to the zoo." At first I did not understand what he was saying, but when he repeated it three times—and then went on to explain there is civil war going on now inside the Soviet Union—I realized that things must be much worse than I had thought.

The Soviet Union *is* in a state of turmoil. In the Caucasus region, martial law has been declared. In Azerbaijan and Armenia, the troops are patrolling. Extreme violence has been used, particularly in Azerbaijan where a demonstration was recently put down. The same kind of thing has been happening in Central Asia—in Uzbekistan, Tajikistan, and Turkestan. In Lithuania, the winners of a recent election openly declared they are urging the state to secede from the Soviet Union, and they are very serious about it. A half-million miners went on strike in July and December of 1989 throughout the Soviet Union, protesting the deterioration in the economy. The Soviet people recognize the magnitude of the economic problems, and they are very worried. The people are now acknowledging things they never acknowledged before, in part because they never had these kinds of problems before.

Not surprisingly, the crime rate is up 40 percent. It is often dangerous for foreigners to be in the streets now. You cannot join a hunting club in the Soviet Union—they are all filled up because membership in a hunting club is the only way a person is legally authorized to buy a rifle. All the weapons have come in from Afghanistan. A local homebred mafia is in control throughout the country. You do not dare call the police.

What surprised me the most is that throughout all of this, the Soviet people are now blaming Gorbachev. What struck me more than anything is that people are actually looking back fondly to the days of Brezhnev.

How did all this come about? It is hard to believe it has only been five years since Gorbachev was elected General Secretary. He came in through the normal channels and served his apprenticeship. He was brought to Moscow by the two most conservative members of the Politburo—Andropov, who was the head of the KGB, and Suslov, who was the head of Ideology. Gorbachev came in and obviously did his work. Why was he picked? Remember the condition in the Politburo in 1985. Everyone was in their 70s or 80s, and many were alcoholics. Gorbachev was the only one who could stand up at 3:00 in the afternoon unaided, so it was by default that he was picked as General Secretary.

When Gorbachev took office, he took an inventory to see what was going on, and you can imagine what he found—that the Soviet Union was the last of the world empires. But it was an empire of problems—Cambodia,

Vietnam, Ethiopia, Nicaragua, and Cuba. The Soviets were fighting in Afghanistan, but there was really nothing to be gained, and they were draining themselves both economically and politically. Military expenditures were 14 to 20 percent of their GNP. They could destroy the United States 60 times over with nuclear weapons, but they did not *need* this capability. We did not need it either, of course, but we could afford such expenditures better than they could. The Soviet central planning system had become counterproductive. The country was producing double the amount of steel that the United States was producing, but what for? It was not doing anything for consumption.

Gorbachev recognized that the society was corrupt all the way to the top. Brezhnev had a passion for fancy cars and women. His daughter was married to the deputy minister of police, who was on the take with the mafia in Uzbekistan—he is now in jail. The daughter was running around with a clown who also smuggled diamonds. If your leadership is that corrupt, you can imagine what was happening all over.

Drunkenness was rampant. I read about committees that had been set up in many factories across the country to prevent workers from coming to work. This might seem like a paradox in an environment when absenteeism was recognized as a problem, but these committees were created because most workers were so drunk, the damage they did at work was worse than their absence.

Gorbachev also recognized that some of the most brilliant people in the country were either exiled or otherwise prevented from contributing to the society.

These factors led to Gorbachev's reform program. He decided to change everything because it was the most counterproductive system you could imagine.

The economy was his first priority. He had a three-pronged program.

1.   He launched the "discipline campaign," with a crackdown on vodka in particular.
2.   He made the machine tool industry his major priority. He assumed that if he built enough machine tools quickly enough, such production would bring about economic reform, the Soviet Union could become the world's largest exporter, enabling them to begin producing consumer goods, and the society would be wonderful. You do not hear that any more, but it was the main point of Gorbachev's strategy for the first two years.
3.   He centralized the government. He was going to create "super-ministries," combinations of several ministries, which would be so big they could not be interfered with at the bottom, and the people at the top would be free to come up with grandiose ideas. What Gorbachev failed to appreciate was that bureaucracies abhor a vacuum and that there was going to be interference at the bottom in any case; and there was.

Although these efforts may have made sense independently, they were a disaster when combined, and they led Gorbachev into some of the problems that he now has to contend with.

Initially, the plan seemed to work. There was growth. People's spirits seemed to be up, and things seemed to be improving. The alcoholism problem was being addressed, there was a new sense of discipline, and everybody seemed to be feeling much better. But then progress hit a wall. Nothing moved.

Gorbachev shifted course. He traveled all over the country and discovered there was enormous alienation. He engaged in give-and-take of the sort that generally leaders around the world do not engage in, and discovered the people were very bitter. They resented the elite Central Committee members because the society seemed to be run for *them*, not for the masses. They had special shops where they could always buy everything, while the masses may have found long lines or no goods at their shops. The elite also had special homes and cars. In fact, in Moscow there is a special lane in the middle of the large boulevards reserved only for the cars of the Central Committee members. The workers' attitudes deteriorated to such an extent that they decided, if they are going to pay us with money they pretend is valuable, then we are going to pretend to work.

Gorbachev realized he had to change things. He introduced a new political structure, creating the Congress of People's Deputies and reducing the power of the party. There would be elections with more than one candidate, and the Supreme Soviet would be elected by the Congress of People's Deputies. This way, the leaders would truly represent the people. Last March when these elections were held in Leningrad, Kiev, and Kharkov, the party leaders ran unopposed, but they lost. It was not an organized campaign, and in some cases when two party members were running against one another they both lost. New elections were then held and in most of these cities reform candidates ran and won and are now the new mayors. Now the deputies come to Moscow with a sense of independence. So far they have maintained their independence, and I think this will continue.

As early as 1987 I knew there would be problems when the process of Glasnost and democratization began to take place. I was visiting Moscow, and while walking in the old part of the city one day I saw a crowd gathered. At the time, it was quite unusual to see that. I approached the man who seemed to be in charge and asked what was going on. He pointed to a tree and said, "Do you see this old elm tree? It is 200 years old and they want to tear it down. Lermontov, the poet, wrote his poems underneath this tree. We cannot let them do it. Sign this petition." I felt like I was back in Harvard Square. I had never heard of a petition before in Moscow. I signed the petition. The tree stands. There is now a fence protecting it.

You can imagine what the party leaders were thinking: Petitions to save trees; what have we come to? If we are going to start worrying about trees, then we will have lost all our power—the next thing you know they are going to start criticizing Stalin! Well, sure enough, they did. And then they started criticizing Lenin as the one who introduced the concentration camps and took away power from the peasants. When you attack Lenin, you attack the guts of the system. If Lenin is vilified, then there is no reason for having the Communist Party in the Soviet Union.

So the system lost its credibility, intellectual rationale, and ideological position. Soon ethnic groups started criticizing each other. This led to the fighting between the Armenians and the Azaris, between one Suni group and a Shiite group, between Sunis and Sunis, and Shiites and Shiites, and everybody against the Russians. Then the government acknowledged that the Nazi-Soviet pact is illegal. For years the Soviet leaders denied that there was such a piece of paper. Finally they found the German variation. Then the *New York Times* announced they found the Russian version, which had been sitting in the files all this time. If the Nazi-Soviet pact is illegal, it means the Baltic states have been coerced into becoming part of the Soviet Union, and they have every right to leave. The same thing goes for Moldavia. Society was breaking up.

Eastern Europe now sees that the gendarme of Europe is gone. Marx called Russia the "gendarme of Europe" because it was the conservative force that put down the 1848 revolution in Hungary and, subsequently, put down the revolutions in Germany, Poland, Czechoslovakia, and again in Hungary. Now, however, Eastern European countries are finding that the Soviet Union is, in effect, saying that they should not be so repressive, and should be more flexible. Eastern Europe has felt the winds of change moving from a more liberal Soviet Union, and the countries are responding by moving toward democracy. History is being made.

The Soviet Union sees all these changes and imports the same political reforms to Eastern Europe. If it is okay to tear down the wall in Berlin separating one Germany from the other, then the Azaris are going to tear down the fence separating the Azaris in Azerbaijan from the Azaris in Iran. The Baltic states are going to call for secession because this is their chance: If they do not get on board now, they may lose the opportunity.

In the face of these momentous changes, you get the feeling that this society is out of control, that it is coming apart, that Gorbachev is presiding over the disintegration not only of the Soviet empire, but all of the U.S.S.R., and he certainly did not have a mandate to do that.

All of this is made worse by the fact that the army now is being discredited. It lost the war in Afghanistan. It harasses young recruits. Draft-dodging is a problem all over the Soviet Union. The fighting in Azerbaijan was led mostly by draftees who defected from the army and moved into the Azaria militia. In the Baltic states people are burning draft cards, burning their uniforms, and picketing in front of army headquarters calling for the end of the occupation of Lithuania.

Despite all of these problems, Perestroika may still work, because Gorbachev has provided an outlet for criticism, something Deng Xiaoping did not do. The Supreme Soviet serves as that outlet. The members of the Supreme Soviet are elected now. So when the people criticize the system, they can criticize their elected leaders and ventilate their frustrations. This is therapeutic. The danger for Gorbachev, however, is that he is now facing hyperventilation because everybody is going overboard in speaking out, and all of these criticisms are made worse by the fact that the economy is rotting.

In fairness to Gorbachev, no matter what he had done, even if he had come up with the right prescription, he probably still would have had problems, because if you attempt to change a society that is as traditional, conservative, and unyielding to change as the Russian one, you know you are going to have a collision.

Let me come back to the three things Gorbachev had in mind with regard to economic reform. Gorbachev focused on machine tools. I do not know why he emphasized machine tools, except to say that the Soviets have a fetish with machine tools. In stressing machine tools, Gorbachev was not able to satisfy the needs of the people. He should have moved to consumer goods and food. Instead, he decided he would increase the output of machine tools, and to do that he would have to take money out of the budget. So he increased expenditures from the national budget.

Gorbachev decided to increase imports of machine tools. Unfortunately, this coincided with a drop in the price of oil in 1985-88. Oil constitutes the Soviet Union's largest hard-currency-earning export (60 percent of the country's hard-currency earnings come from the sale of oil). Because of the drop in the price of oil, the Soviet Union's hard-currency revenues from oil fell by one-third. So Gorbachev found himself constricted because of the decrease in hard-currency earnings—his convertible currency earnings. Meanwhile, though, he had increased the importation of machine tools. To compensate, he decided to cut back on the importation of consumer goods.

The decrease in imports of consumer goods was not enough to match the fall in oil revenues. In fact, a budget deficit resulted. The budget deficit in 1985 was 18 billion rubles. In 1986 it rose to 48 billion rubles, over a twofold increase. Last year the budget deficit was 100 to 120 billion rubles—the equivalent of 12 to 14 percent of GNP. You can see what a desperate situation this is when you consider how worried we are in the United States about our own budget deficit, which is actually a comparatively small 3 to 4 percent of GNP.

The Soviets financed this enormous deficit the old-fashioned way—by printing money. This, of course, created inflation. The Soviets now have inflation of at least 20 percent a year. It also reduced the standard of living as people protected themselves by buying gold, jewelry, antiques, appliances, furniture, television sets, and watches—everybody hoarded. Then because things were in such short supply, the country's standard of living began to fall. The real per capita income declined, and soon the real income declined as well.

Another part of Gorbachev's plan was to try to alleviate the alcoholism problem by restricting the supply, and therefore the consumption, of vodka. What he did not appreciate was that vodka generated 10 to 20 percent of the Soviet Union's budget revenues. Also, after about a year of significantly decreased supply of their favorite beverage, the Soviet population started making moonshine. To make moonshine, however, you need sugar. The demand created a sugar shortage, which led to rationing for the first time since World War II.

To fight all of these new problems, Gorbachev came up with three solutions, which on the surface made sense, but because they were obstructed by bureaucratic red tape are not working. In 1987-88 he introduced cooperatives and private trade, but because there were so many strings attached, only a few people could actually set up their own businesses. Thus, prices went up because there were not enough of these entities to be competitive, and those that existed began to take advantage of the situation. Shortages ensued because the operators of these businesses took goods where there was abundant supply and moved them to areas where they could get a higher price. The local mafia took over because the cooperatives were making so much money. The police either could not cope with this kind of problem or were bribed by the mafia to participate.

In addition to encouraging private trade, Gorbachev decided to authorize family farming, similar to what took place in China. The private farmers are hesitant because family farming does not have a long tradition inside the Soviet Union. Again, to give Gorbachev some credit, this is not only a problem of communism, it is a historic problem that goes back to the czars.

Gorbachev then tried to set up joint ventures with foreign partners. These ventures are also being criticized because they are obstructed by bureaucrats; as a result, only 100 of 1,300 joint ventures actually work. These ventures cannot get convertible currency, so the only ventures that are successful are the ones in the business of extracting raw materials such as oil and natural gas.

Meanwhile, the economy continues to deteriorate. The GNP is dropping. The ruble has lost its value. They will not sell you goods in the Baltic states unless you can prove you live in the Baltic states. In Leningrad it became impossible to buy food in the shops unless you could prove that you lived in Leningrad. The Baltic states are talking about issuing their own currency because the ruble has lost all credibility. The society is disintegrating. Last November they announced a return to central planning, they have announced a return to price control, and they have closed down some of the cooperatives because they were making too much money. Throughout there is this feeling that no one is in charge—no one knows what to do.

Trying to change a society that is this deeply grounded and traditional is difficult, particularly in a short period of time. But the problem is that if Gorbachev cannot produce immediate results, the people are going to lose their patience, and this is beginning to happen. What Gorbachev has managed to produce is a remarkable form of openness and democratization, the kinds of things that make your heart beat faster because they are so exciting. The economic reforms, however, are not taking hold. Perestroika is not working.

Question and Answer Session

Question: What happened when Brezhnev, Andropov, and some of the other leaders came in? Did they not find the same problems that Gorbachev found?

Goldman: Well, Andropov began to talk about economic change, although he did not talk about Glasnost. In fact, under Andropov, the political situation was the most stringent it had ever been. All forms of dissent were wiped out. Khrushchev had been an experimenter. Brezhnev was brought in to settle things down, and he did. Under Brezhnev, once you were made a party official, you stayed there until you died. It was a little bit like academic tenure. It did not matter what you did. You just kind of stayed there and rotted. That is one of the reasons for the changes under Gorbachev. Unfortunately, economic reform continued to deteriorate under these new circumstances.

Question: Can the Soviets establish the value of the ruble without tying it to gold?

Goldman: I don't know. What they must have is a monetary reform of the sort they had in 1947, but they have been unwilling to do that. Even if they tie the currency to gold, they worry that the gold will all simply disappear, and at least now they have something they can hold on to for dear life. So, they have been very conservative about it. Gold is kind of like their last legacy, their inheritance. I don't see what they can do now unless they have a massive series of changes, destroy the money situation, come up with a brand-new currency, and institute price control. But that would be politically disruptive. It is very interesting to contrast what is happening in the Soviet Union now with what is happening in Poland, where radical change is taking place. As of January 1, Poland went for broke, letting prices seek their own level, having convertibility, stopping the subsidies from the budget. These changes do seem to be improving the Polish economy a little bit. The question is whether there will be enough improvement to prevent or to offset the growing unemployment that is occurring and to make the people feel that there is hope over the horizon. What is happening now is that people in Poland are being patient because it is a honeymoon era, because Solidarity has just taken over. The honeymoon is over in the Soviet Union. Gorbachev has had five years, and he produced the wrong kinds of things.

Question: What happens when patience is exhausted in the Soviet Union?

Goldman: I don't know. We have seen examples of this already. At the end of December there was rioting—food riots started by vodka riots. Patience is wearing thin in the different republics. Gorbachev, however, is a master politician of the sort that I cannot imagine anyplace else. I cannot conceive of a chief executive officer who would preside over a situation in which internally everything began to disintegrate and yet he would still be there after five years. But Gorbachev manages to push aside his opponents, just as he managed to push through a new provision whereby he will be elected president of the whole country, not by a national election which will take place four years from now, but by the Congress of People's Deputies. There are some who say that this is wrong because it gives him too much power and it will bring back the cult of the personality that existed under Stalin. The debate over this was furious. People were bitter and critical of Gorbachev, and he responded in kind. And they are frightened now that indeed this is the cult of the personality, that he is falling back into the old patterns.

Question: Can a possible solution be to break up the country into smaller republics, getting it to a smaller scale?

Goldman: That could happen. Each of the different republics seems to be splintering now. Even the Ukraine people are beginning to talk about seceding. It does not make sense, however, from the point of view of many of the republics. The Baltic states, which are the most advanced in this kind of thing, are very small. The smallest is Estonia, with a million and a half people. The largest is Lithuania, with three and a half million people. It would be like having Boston form its own country. I don't think it makes much sense, because the market and work force are so small, but many people do. They feel that, as bad as things may be, if they do it on their own they will be like a Finland or Sweden; it is better than being stuck within the Soviet Union. They don't find anything attractive about the new system.

Question: In other instances in history when a country had internal problems, they would try to distract attention by creating an external diversion. Do you think the Soviets might do this?

Goldman: That is possible, but right now I think it is unlikely. What is remarkable, in fact, is that Gorbachev seems to be so yielding and is doing everything he can to cut back the Soviet empire. He is cutting military expenditures at home and reducing support outside. One of the problems in Nicaragua is that Gorbachev has cut back. He is cutting back in Cuba in the same way. The military itself is in chaos. They are very upset that they are being demobilized. They have lost their jobs and cannot get others. Many of the former soldiers do not have a place to live. The answer to this question is very dangerous to predict because everything is changing so quickly.

Question: Should the policy toward the republics be dictated by economic needs, raw material needs, and so on?

Goldman: Well, it should be, but when you are in your romantic stage, nothing stands in your way. The Soviets are telling the Baltic states, "If you secede we are going to take away your oil. We are going to charge you higher prices." And the Soviets are already beginning to put the squeeze on. They are freezing bank accounts. They have jacked up the price of oil to let the Baltic states know that they are going to have to pay more. What has happened, of course, in the case of Azerbaijan, which is where they produce a small amount of oil but produce a good portion of the oil equipment, is that production has now been disrupted. This is also happening in coal mining. Also, the railroad industry is in chaos. Goods are not being delivered. Because of the strikes, production figures are now dropping in these industries, and there should be problems. I think those problems are going to continue to occur until people have enough faith in the system to feel that it is worthwhile.

Question: What is the best policy for the United States to have regarding the Soviet Union?

Goldman: Last week I was talking to one of my friends in the National Security Council about Bush's policy, which on the whole I think is now coming along better. I said one of the best things we could have done in terms of the policy was to announce that we will limit our troops in Europe to 195,000, because that allows Gorbachev to reduce his troops. It also lets him save face because he is being thrown out of Eastern Europe in any case, and I do not even know where they are going to keep the 195,000 troops they have there because nobody wants them. But having done that, why did the administration then say, "Well, we want an extra 30,000 around the periphery." That destroys parity and takes us back to an advantageous position again, something the Soviets have just given up and are very upset about.

I asked my friend, "Why did you do that?" And she said, "Well, they were not supposed to agree to that. This was a kind of bidding process, and we just threw that in, and in three days, they said 'yes.'" My response was, "Well, you have to realize that, because Gorbachev is so hard pushed, he has to take anything that is put on his plate." And that is dangerous. It is dangerous for him, and it is dangerous for us. When we negotiate with this man now, we should do things not for bidding purposes, not for bargaining purposes, but for reaching a sustainable compromise. And that is the kind of thing we can do economically. A Marshall Plan is impossible. The problems must be solved within the Soviet Union. The focus must be on arms control, absorbing the soldiers who are being demobilized, converting industry, and cutting back on their budget.